"I am so excited about *Creative Teaching in Counselor Education and Supervision*! It will empower our program by strengthening passion, creativity, and professional identity in our counselor education students and faculty. I hope it will help me grow alongside my students and colleagues in new ways, just as learning in higher education should."

—**Jan Powers**, PhD, *Assistant Professor and Program Director at Creighton University*

"This is a must-read for all counselor educators. It encourages counselor education that is relevant, interesting, and inventive. To mold students with a creative twist is not only good for educators and their students but also for their future counseling clients."

—**Dale V. Wayman**, PhD, *licensed Clinical Addictions Counselor, licensed Mental Health Counselor, and approved Clinical Supervisor at Capella University*

"*Creative Teaching in Counselor Education and Supervision* is an engaging text that focuses on providing strategies and methods for educators that are much needed in the profession. Throughout the text, readers use self-reflection and learn practical strategies that can be implemented easily into any educator's teaching."

—**Marguerite Ohrtman**, EdD, *Program Director of Counselor Education at the University of Minnesota*

"This book is an essential resource for counselor educators looking to enhance their andragogical practice. The book's emphasis on imaginative and inventive techniques in teaching sets it apart, ensuring its relevance to counselor educators committed to fostering innovative change in their curriculum."

—**Tracie Rutherford Self**, PhD, *Associate Professor at Minnesota State University, Mankato*

"*Creative Teaching in Counselor Education and Supervision* is vital reading for counselor educators seeking to enhance engagement and foster innovative learning experiences. Packed with practical strategies and creative techniques, this book inspires educators to elevate their teaching across diverse instructional formats."

—**Treye Rosenberger, PhD, LMHC(IA), LPC(TX), CRC, NCC,** *ACS Department Chair, Assistant Professor in the Department of Counselor Education Programs*

Creative Teaching in Counselor Education and Supervision

Creative Teaching in Counselor Education and Supervision offers a fresh perspective on teaching in counselor education and related helping fields. Tailored for educators who want to invigorate their instructional approaches, this book is a valuable resource packed with creative strategies and techniques.

With a focus on practical applications, *Creative Teaching in Counselor Education and Supervision* empowers educators to elevate their teaching methodologies. It provides tools for fostering engagement, critical thinking, and hands-on learning, with an emphasis on adapting techniques for various instructional formats, including online, hybrid, in-person, and residency-style programs.

Casey E. Baker, EdD, LMHC, RPT-S, is a Core Faculty Member at Capella University. As a trained play therapist and counselor educator, Baker has focused her career on making learning environments active, innovative, and creative.

Rebecca Sametz Riddle, PhD, CRC, NCC, LPC, is a Core Faculty Member at Capella University. She focuses on youth with disabilities, family support, workforce readiness, employer needs, and psychosocial adjustment for individuals and veterans.

Lynn O'Brien, EdD, LPCC, LMHC, RPT, NCC, is an Assistant Professor at Capella University. With experience as a clinician, school counselor, and counselor educator, O'Brien builds relationships and nurtures development and growth through strength-based and experiential activities.

Blair Sumner Vincent, PhD, NCC, in her role as an Academic Director, is tasked with overseeing innovation strategies. She consistently evaluates emerging strategies, software solutions, and educational approaches. She aims to continually challenge and reshape the landscape of higher education.

Creative Teaching in Counselor Education and Supervision

Casey E. Baker, Rebecca Sametz Riddle, Lynn O'Brien, and Blair Sumner Vincent

Routledge
Taylor & Francis Group

NEW YORK AND LONDON

Designed cover image: Getty Images

First published 2026
by Routledge
605 Third Avenue, New York, NY 10158

and by Routledge
4 Park Square, Milton Park, Abingdon, Oxon, OX14 4RN

Routledge is an imprint of the Taylor & Francis Group, an informa business

© 2026 Casey E. Baker, Rebecca Sametz Riddle, Lynn O'Brien, and Blair Sumner Vincent

The right of Casey E. Baker, Rebecca Sametz Riddle, Lynn O'Brien, and Blair Sumner Vincent to be identified as authors of this work has been asserted in accordance with sections 77 and 78 of the Copyright, Designs and Patents Act 1988.

ISBN: 978-1-032-84738-2 (hbk)
ISBN: 978-1-032-84736-8 (pbk)
ISBN: 978-1-003-51471-8 (ebk)

DOI: 10.4324/9781003514718

Typeset in Adobe Caslon Pro
by Deanta Global Publishing Services, Chennai, India

CONTENTS

INTRODUCTION

This book began as a spark, a comment in a group chat, a moment of laughter in supervision, a student's bold idea shared in class. That spark has grown into a campfire of creativity, fueled by the energy, passion, and curiosity of the people we have had the privilege of learning alongside. Whether it was a student courageously demonstrating a mock session, a colleague dreaming up an unconventional assignment, or a client making meaning through metaphor, we have been continually reminded that creativity is not just an accessory to counselor education—it is the heartbeat.

Much of that heartbeat grew louder and stronger during our countless hours planning in-person counseling residencies at our shared institution. We imagined themed sessions like "Finding Our Way" in a camping-style residency complete with trail maps and patches. Superhero-themed residencies where students discovered their counseling powers and crafted origin stories of their professional identity. These residencies were where magic and meaning collided, and our friendship blossomed. Moving from colleagues to friends.

But let's be honest, it has not always been easy to be the ones doing things differently. Embracing creativity often meant overcoming that small voice that whispered, *You look ridiculous*, or navigating the raised eyebrows that came with coloring outside the traditional lines of academia. We have felt the pressure to conform, questioning "Is this rigorous enough?" and the challenge of standing by unconventional choices when others preferred the safety of structure. There were moments when the energy in the room was so high, the laughter so loud, that someone would jokingly say, *You can't possibly be having that much fun and still be teaching something.* And still, we leaned in. Because every time we saw a student light up with insight or a classroom shift from fearful to free, we were reminded: this work matters.

The most powerful part was not just seeing students light up; it was watching our colleagues step in with capes of their own, adding their brilliance, building on the themes, and showing that counselor education can be deeply human, wildly creative, and seriously fun. Those moments, where educators inspired one another to be different, to take risks, and to lead with authenticity, became the heart of this book.

This book is for anyone who's ever asked, *Can we do this differently?* and dared to try. It is for counselor educators who infuse life into lesson plans, see their classrooms as playgrounds for growth, and understand that creativity is not about being flashy but about being real. It is for students learning to trust their instincts, supervisors who guide with structure and imagination, and anyone who believes that meaningful learning happens when we color outside the lines.

As counselor educators, we often ask students to approach their work with curiosity, openness, and adaptability. This book reflects that same invitation. It is a call to embrace creativity's powerful and sometimes unpredictable nature, not just as a technique but as a guiding philosophy. Creative approaches help learners access insight, feel seen, and explore counseling possibilities beyond the traditional frame, whether it takes the form of metaphor, art, storytelling, movement, or play.

We did not write this book to offer a rigid formula. Instead, we offer a collection of creative possibilities—activities, reflections, and teaching tools meant to inspire, adapt, and evolve with you. Let this be your trail map, your toolkit, your campfire stories passed from one generation of counselor educators to the next. Let it ignite your belief that doing things differently is essential.

ACKNOWLEDGMENTS

To the colleagues who said "yes" when we asked for your favorite creative activities, thank you for sharing your brilliance and reminding us that inspiration grows best in community. Your contributions gave this book its heartbeat.

To our students, the true adventurers in this journey, thank you for your courage to try, stumble, reflect, and rise again. Trusting us to be your guides on your journey.

To our mentors and fellow dreamers, thank you for reminding us that joy, wonder, and curiosity belong in academia. You have helped us keep the magic alive.

Here's to doing it differently, with purpose, with playfulness, and with plenty of room for glitter, growth, and grace.

1

THE ROLE OF CREATIVITY IN COUNSELOR EDUCATION

A GUIDE FOR PURPOSEFUL IMPLEMENTATION

How does one cultivate creativity? What images or ideas come to mind? Maybe it is painting a picture, writing a song, or designing something new and innovative. Now, shift that lens and consider what it means to be a creative counselor educator. Do you think of aspects like designing innovative lesson plans? Or potentially incorporating expressive arts into the learning process? Maybe even using one of your favorite children's stories to illustrate complex concepts. Could creativity look like an educator engaging with students in a way that fosters safety and openness where students feel encouraged to explore new perspectives?

Take a few minutes and jot down your thoughts: What does being a creative counselor educator look like to you? Are there any questions, concerns, or excitement that surface? Are there barriers that keep coming up, such as doubts about your creativity or concerns about time or resources? Are you saying to yourself, I am the least creative person ever? As you continue through the upcoming chapters, revisit these reflections and consider how your understanding of creativity might evolve.

    DOI: 10.4324/9781003514718-1

Creativity as an Essential Framework in Counselor Education

While creativity is often recognized as essential in the counseling process, its integration into counselor education is frequently limited to specific methods or courses, such as those focused on play therapy and child counseling (Coaston & Lawrence, 2019; Lawrence et al., 2015). This limited integration misses the opportunity to view creativity as an essential framework for teaching all counselor education courses. Rather than viewing creativity in isolated coursework, it should be understood as an interactive, dynamic process spread across the curriculum (Lin, 2011).

Creativity in education requires more than innovative lesson plans or engaging classroom activities; it demands a pedagogical approach that integrates creative teaching, teaching for creativity, and creative learning (Lin, 2011). Creative teaching involves imaginative methods to make learning more engaging and meaningful, which are often shaped by educators' past experiences, risk-taking, and commitment to experiential approaches (McGhee et al., 2019). Teaching for creativity fosters students' ability to think divergently, explore possibilities, and develop independent thought (Lin, 2011). Creative learning, the final element, ensures that students actively engage in inquiry, problem-solving, and collaboration rather than passively absorbing information, building essential skills that any counselor educator would want to see in a future counselor.

An example of this integration is the *Theory sale*, discussed in Chapter 5, which can be implemented in any theory content-related course. The authors utilize an in-class activity where students work in groups to "sell" a particular counseling theory to their peers with the goal of "recruiting" others to their chosen theory. Each group is randomly given a theory; they work to develop a persuasive presentation and create materials that highlight the theory's strengths, unique aspects, and practical applications.

In this process, students must engage actively with the content and one another. They work to articulate their understanding and build on each other's ideas. Discussions can be lively as students evaluate the merits of competing theories, question their assumptions, and debate perspectives. This activity promotes critical thinking and flexibility as students must tailor their presentations to appeal to their audience, using creative methods to convey complex ideas in an engaging and accessible way.

Students have demonstrated this by fully embracing their role as "used car salesmen," employing humor, enthusiasm, and strategic persuasion to convince their classmates to adopt their assigned theory. Some have crafted slogans, jingles, and even skits to highlight the advantages of their perspective. For example, a group selling Person-Centered Therapy once used a no-pressure sales pitch offering "Free acceptance with every purchase." Another group selling Cognitive Behavioral Therapy created an infomercial-style presentation with testimonials from satisfied clients whose thinking patterns have been transformed. Spoken word poems exploring themes of freedom, responsibility, and the search for meaning to represent existential therapy have been truly powerful. These creative expressions deepen students' engagement, allowing them to connect with the core tenets of the theory.

Andragogy and Creativity

In activities discussed in this book, students learn how to collaborate more effectively, negotiate differing viewpoints, and present ideas persuasively using creative teaching methods. This collaborative learning is common among adults in education. This way of learning encourages diverse perspectives, which fosters a creative exchange of ideas and possibly innovative solutions.

Andragogy, popularized by Malcolm Knowles (1968), emphasizes that adults learn differently from children, and it supports creativity in teaching by focusing on key principles that engage and empower adults. Andragogy builds on prior experience, enhanced through collaborative and peer-based learning opportunities. Creativity plays an important role in this approach, allowing students to connect their past experiences to their new knowledge in a more personal way (Lin, 2011). For example, in a group dynamics role play, students take on different group members' roles (e.g., monopolizer, silent member, scapegoat) and reflect on how these dynamics influence the group process. Drawing from their experience and observations, they gain deeper insight into effective facilitation strategies and the complexities of group counseling.

As students engage in creative activities, they not only deepen their comprehension but also build a strong sense of mutual support. Shared experiences foster connections that extend beyond the classroom, creating a professional network rooted in trust and collaboration. Students approach new concepts from multiple perspectives by integrating their wealth of personal and professional experience, enhancing their problem-solving and critical-thinking skills. When educators recognize and actively incorporate these diverse experiences into the curriculum, they cultivate a richer, more inclusive learning environment. Through storytelling, reflection, and experiential learning, students broaden their viewpoints, challenge assumptions, and leave the classroom more empowered to apply their knowledge in real-world settings.

An activity discussed in Chapter 5, *Exploring My Racial, Ethnic, and Cultural Identity*, illustrates how creative teaching can foster both self-awareness and professional growth. This activity blends self-reflection with actionable insights, encouraging students to critically examine their identities while equipping them with tools to advance cultural competence and advocate for social justice in their future roles. Through thoughtful exploration and guided discussion, students are able to connect past experiences with new learning in meaningful and personal ways.

Creative teaching methods—such as project-based learning, experiential activities, and multimodal approaches using art, technology, or storytelling—offer students multiple entry points for engagement. Activities like the one above exemplify how creativity enhances andragogical principles by promoting flexible, personalized learning environments that honor students' interests, experiences, and schedules. To support this flexibility, each activity featured in this book includes a section outlining how it can be adapted for various learning contexts.

Another essential element in supporting adult learning is reflection. Reflection invites students to think deeply about their learning, explore alternative perspectives, and challenge their assumptions (Rothwell, 2024). Creative reflection methods—such as journaling, peer feedback, and group discussions—not only deepen understanding but also help students internalize and apply what they've learned. This ongoing engagement with reflection nurtures creativity over time. As students are encouraged to explore new ideas and diverse methods of expression, they remain curious and open-minded learners (Lin, 2011). To support this process, every activity in this book is paired with debriefing questions designed to spark meaningful reflection and dialogue.

The Ripple Effect of Creativity in Counselor Education

As has been discussed, creativity enhances and strengthens adaptability and problem-solving skills, both of which are important in navigating life stressors, including those that may come from graduate school (Lawrence et al., 2015). When creativity is embedded in learning, students report an increased understanding of course content and a strong sense of professional counselor identity (Duffy et al., 2020). Research in higher education further highlights a positive relationship between instructors' creativity in the classroom and students' perceptions of instructor effectiveness and their creative thinking abilities after the course (Milgram & Davidovich, 2010). In short, fostering creativity in the classroom benefits both the learning process and students' professional growth.

Beyond enhancing comprehension, creativity introduces an element of uncertainty and exploration that promotes student growth. Unlike traditional methods, creative activities often encourage multiple perspectives and diverse problem-solving approaches. This openness encourages students to take intellectual risks and embrace learning as an iterative process. As a result, students become more confident in their ability to generate innovative solutions, a critical skill for counselors who must navigate complex client needs with flexibility and insight.

This shift to exploration can lead to a ripple effect where students develop the ability to adapt, innovate, and approach challenges with flexibility while in the field. As future counselors, students who have honed their creative skills will be better prepared to tailor interventions to support their clients. They will be able to think critically about their cases. This approach enhances the students' professional development and positively contributes to the culture of the counseling profession.

Cultivating a Culture of Creativity

This ripple effect extends beyond individual courses, influencing the wider academic and professional community. Self-care is a key area where creativity can be deeply integrated across the curriculum. Given the emotional demands of the counseling profession, self-care is not just beneficial but essential, and when approached creatively, it becomes even more impactful. Researchers emphasized the importance of embedding self-compassion and self-care throughout counselor education programs rather than treating them as optional discussions (Coaston & Lawrence, 2019). Some simple ways programs can get started are by implementing self-care plans into assignments or program requirements, offering workshops or seminars focusing on the role of these skills in professional and personal lives. Additionally, having a self-care mentorship program can offer great mutual support.

Embracing creativity at an institutional level requires intentionality and openness to innovation.

By modeling and prioritizing creative thinking, educators inspire not only their students but also their colleagues. This model helps shift creativity from being viewed as an abstract or optional element of education to a fundamental component of effective teaching and learning.

Launching creativity initiatives requires thoughtful planning and alignment with program goals, resources, and the unique needs of students. Before implementation, educators should consider factors such as institutional support, faculty buy-in, and student engagement strategies that ensure that creative practices are sustainable and impactful. The remainder of this chapter serves as a practical guide for implementing creativity in counselor education, offering educators concrete strategies and adaptive activities that can transform both the classroom experience and the broader professional landscape.

A Guide for Purposeful Implementation

One of the central roles of counselor educators is to design and facilitate learning experiences that not only deliver knowledge but also cultivate critical thinking, professional identity, and personal growth in future counselors. Teaching in counselor education should be approached with the same intentionality and ethical grounding as clinical work (Malott et al., 2014). Incorporating creative measures into teaching should be intentional and guided by a clear understanding of one's personal teaching philosophy and standards. This philosophy should consider the factors and processes that effectively promote learning and skill development. To maximize learning, purposeful implementation should be approached as a developmental process that occurs over time and incorporates diverse modalities (Gladding & Casares, 2022). Regardless of the course, topic, or skill being taught, educators should adopt a stance of purposeful implementation when incorporating creative activities. The following guide offers considerations to assist educators in this process.

Teaching Philosophy

While in one's doctoral program, future counselor educators are beginning to develop and hone in on their teaching philosophy. Like the development of counseling theories, crafting a teaching philosophy involves blending personal insights with teaching strategies and theories (Halbur & Halbur, 2015; Kearns & Sullivan, 2011; Medina & Draugalis, 2013). A teaching philosophy provides the foundation for intentional and reflective teaching practices. It allows educators to articulate their core beliefs about learning, counseling, and professional development, creating a consistent framework for student interaction (Hall et al., 2021).

Emerging research suggests that teaching philosophy can influence not only how we teach but also what we teach. Moe et al. (2022) found that counselor educators who identify adult education as a foundational part of their teaching philosophy are more likely to include LGBTQ issues across counseling curricula. This finding reinforces the practical impact of teaching philosophy: educators who adopt adult learning principles—such as learner collaboration, relevance to lived experience, and empowerment through knowledge—may be more attuned to integrating topics that reflect client diversity and sociocultural realities. While other philosophies like critical pedagogy, experiential learning, and constructivism were positively associated with LGBTQ coverage, adult education philosophy was the most significant predictor of curricular integration.

This research highlights the value of aligning teaching philosophy with inclusive, equity-focused content. Counselor educators committed to social justice and multicultural competence may find that reflecting on and articulating their teaching values can serve as a catalyst for more inclusive pedagogy. Teaching philosophy becomes not just a tool for personal clarity, but a mechanism for systemic impact—shaping how students encounter and explore complex issues like identity, power, and privilege in the counseling relationship.

If you are revisiting or developing your teaching philosophy, begin with reflection. Consider journaling about the values that guide your work. What inspired you to pursue counselor education? What kind of classroom environment do you want to foster? How do you define effective teaching, especially in diverse and evolving cultural contexts? Then, explore different educational theories—such as adult education or constructivism—and consider how they align with or challenge your current approach. Use this integration to shape a teaching statement that not only reflects your goals and beliefs but also guides your decisions about content, including critical areas like LGBTQ-affirming practices.

Next, explore relevant teaching theories and assess whether they align with or challenge your current beliefs or practices. This book does not advocate for a single right theory, as theory exploration and integration are deeply personal processes for each educator. Take time to engage with different theories and reflect on how they connect with your insights from the previous section. Do they support your existing perspectives or push you to think differently about your approach? A helpful starting point is to create a brief vision statement that captures your educational goals and aspirations. This statement should reflect how you aim to influence students and contribute to the counseling profession.

Then, using your reflections and theoretical exploration, begin to draft or revise your teaching philosophy statement. There are various ways to structure your statement, but a simple method can include an introduction where you provide an overview of yourself, including your vision statement and your overall goal as an educator. Next, spend some time discussing how specific teaching theories influence your approach, and provide examples of how the integration of your goal as an educator and theories translates into your teaching practices. Lastly, reflect on and discuss your commitment to growth as an educator.

Collaboration, reflection, and revision are the last steps in this process (West et al., 2021). Do not neglect this step. Share your draft with a colleague or peer, and encourage them to assess areas of your philosophy, including theoretical integration. Reflect on the feedback and identify areas for improvement or further exploration. Revise your statement regularly to ensure it evolves with your professional growth and changing student needs. To help you remember, set it as a goal to review regularly in your professional development plan.

Standards Check

After developing their teaching philosophy, counselor educators must ensure that their creative approaches align with course-specific, programmatic, and accreditation standards. Clearly articulated learning objectives and explaining the rationale behind course activities at the beginning of each lesson help students understand how these activities connect to broader course goals and professional competencies. Rather than viewing standards as barriers to creativity, counselor educators can use them as a framework that supports innovation.

Accreditation is critical in maintaining the rigor and credibility of a counselor's education programs. It ensures that students receive a quality education that meets the expectations of the profession and prepares them for licensure and ethical practice. While accreditation standards may appear rigid, they do not inherently restrict creativity. In fact, counselor educators can leverage these standards as springboards for creative pedagogy by designing assignments and activities that simultaneously meet required competencies and foster student engagement.

To effectively tailor educational activities to accreditation and program standards, counselor educators can follow a structured process that begins with identifying the relevant standards. This includes reviewing the Council for Accreditation of Counseling and Related Educational Programs (CACREP) standards, program-level objectives, and specific course learning outcomes. Educators can find these resources through their departmental accreditation documentation, CACREP website, course syllabi, and curriculum guides.

Once the relevant standards are identified, the next step is to break them down into teachable concepts. Because accreditation language can be broad or technical, educators should translate this into digestible components that guide lesson planning. For example, a CACREP standard related to multicultural and pluralistic characteristics might be broken down into key concepts like cultural identity, systems of privilege and oppression, and worldview development.

To ensure transparency and accountability, educators should then map each activity to the relevant learning objectives and standards. This can be done in the form of a table or checklist, making it easier to track alignment. Learning objectives are provided for each activity in this book.

Foster a Safe and Collaborative Learning Environment

Effective teaching is rooted in the development of a supportive and motivating learning environment. Interpersonal factors such as instructor enthusiasm, warmth, and immediacy are essential components of student engagement and satisfaction (Malott et al., 2014). These qualities naturally lend themselves to creative teaching approaches. When educators use humor, storytelling, or imaginative activities, they create relational classrooms that mirror the therapeutic alliance—a parallel process that supports counselor identity development.

With any activity, educators must consider both the physical and emotional risks and the accessibility for all students. Educators play an essential role in creating a safe and collaborative learning environment (Swank & Houseknecht, 2019). Key considerations include ensuring equitable access to technology, programs, and resources, addressing environmental factors such as classroom space and comfort, and being mindful of financial barriers.

Additionally, educators should be aware of any specific needs or concerns that may arise based on their students' diverse backgrounds and experiences. Educators encourage diversity of thought and experience by acknowledging and celebrating the varied perspectives, cultures, and experiences students bring to the classroom. This involves using culturally sensitive language, incorporating diverse examples, and creating relevant content that resonates with students from various cultural perspectives. Effective facilitation requires creating psychologically safe environments where diverse perspectives are welcomed and students feel heard and supported (Swank & Houseknecht, 2019).

At the program level, a protocol should be established to address situations where students may feel uncomfortable or distressed during the learning experience. This protocol should be reviewed and updated regularly to ensure its effectiveness and alignment with best practices.

A sample protocol is included in Appendix A. Furthermore, faculty should regularly supervise or consult to reflect on curriculum implementation and other important concerns. This supervision can create a supportive environment by enhancing both faculty development and student well-being.

At the beginning of any course, educators should engage students in a discussion about safety protocols and agreed-upon classroom rules. Establishing this structure is essential for fostering a safe and collaborative learning environment. These protocols should be easily accessible to all students and regularly updated, whether posted online or displayed in the physical classroom.

To reinforce these expectations, the author incorporates a check-out self-assessment in both in-person and online courses. This assessment includes a question prompting students to reflect on and rate their ability to uphold classroom rules and expectations, encouraging ongoing awareness and accountability.

Structure and Student Needs

The Universal Design for Learning (UDL) framework (CAST, 2024) provides educators with a dynamic approach to fostering inclusivity, accessibility, and creativity in their teaching. UDL encourages flexibility in presenting information and highlights the importance of reducing barriers so all students can effectively acquire knowledge and skills (Bills, 2021; Wilde & Banik, 2025). By incorporating creativity into the UDL framework, educators can design innovative learning experiences that engage students, such as integrating visual arts, role-playing, or multimedia projects to deepen understanding and enhance critical thinking.

Incorporating creativity within the UDL framework allows educators to present material through multiple formats, empowering students to engage with content that aligns with their unique strengths and learning styles. Similarly, students are encouraged to express their understanding in varied and imaginative ways, such as crafting reflective narratives, designing group presentations, or developing creative metaphors to conceptualize counseling theories. By blending UDL principles with creative teaching methods, counselor educators not only enhance accessibility but also inspire students to think divergently and approach challenges with an open and flexible mindset.

Educators must also balance creativity, structure, and student developmental needs when designing and implementing programs. Balance in counselor education is particularly critical, as students are developing both their professional identity and counseling skills. Scholars emphasize the need for intentional scaffolding to ensure developmentally appropriate learning activities (McAuliffe & Eriksen, 2019). Understanding the timing of courses within a program is essential to meeting students where they are. Beginning-level courses benefit from a more structured and supportive environment emphasizing foundational counseling skills and ethical awareness (Field et al., 2022). These courses should incorporate creative activities with a high degree of guidance, such as guided role plays or structured reflection prompts, to help students build confidence and competency. In contrast, more advanced courses—such as practicum, internship, and clinical seminars—can invite more open-ended, complex, and exploratory approaches to learning.

Another key element of applying UDL effectively is providing diverse opportunities for participation, as students often engage with material and skill sets in different ways. For instance, some students may excel in verbal discussions, while others favor written reflections or collaborative digital tools. Educators can utilize strategies such as check-out reflections and dyad or triad discussions to encourage authentic engagement. It is also important to consider students' varying levels of comfort with participation. Some may need more time for reflection, while others require more active engagement. Checking in during the next class or later in the week provides continued support for those who process information at a different pace. This ability to respond to individual needs while maintaining appropriate structure helps students gradually build confidence and mastery.

During classroom activities, educators should remain actively engaged—circulating in the classroom or joining breakout rooms and discussion boards—to assess student understanding in real time. Pausing periodically to check for comprehension allows educators to identify whether students need additional support, scaffolding, or a shift in instruction. This flexibility and responsiveness are vital when working with diverse learners in a creative environment. Educators must be able to adapt instruction in the moment—responding to student developmental needs, pacing challenges, or emerging classroom dynamics (Swank & Houseknecht, 2019).

Educators can also foster engagement and inclusion by designing personally meaningful activities. Making learning relevant to students' lived experiences—whether from personal, academic, or professional backgrounds—helps bridge the gap between theory and practice. Since many students in counseling programs bring rich life experiences into the classroom, educators should encourage them to draw on these strengths through storytelling, peer teaching, or real-world case examples. This deepens engagement and validates the diverse perspectives students bring to the learning process.

Finally, in the rapidly evolving landscape of educational technology, counselor educators must be mindful of students' varying levels of digital fluency. To ensure equitable access, educators should provide clear instructions, offer tutorials when introducing new tools, and ensure that all content is accessible in multiple formats. By taking a proactive, inclusive approach to digital integration, educators can increase students' confidence and promote the creative use of technology in the service of learning and professional growth.

Debriefing Session

A structured debriefing session should follow every activity. These will allow students to share insights and learn from each other, highlighting the importance of diverse experiences and peer learning. This is an essential moment to connect the creative work back to clinical practice and allow students to reflect on what they have learned through the experience. Educators can encourage students to question assumptions, explore different perspectives, and engage deeply with the activity. Techniques such as reflective journaling, group discussions, or individual feedback sessions can facilitate this process. Further, it is beneficial to revisit reflections in the subsequent classes to offer students additional opportunities to share their insights.

In the second half of this book, we share activities we've used and contributions from other professionals in the field. Each activity includes a set of debriefing questions to help guide the session. While these questions help structure the debriefing of the activity, it's important to stay attuned to your students' needs. They may have gained insights that require further exploration. Each time you use an activity, it will offer a unique experience and may need different adjustments. These can be implemented as an in-class discussion, reflective papers, discussion boards, artmaking, or any other means of reflection.

Evaluating Outcomes

Counselor educators must be willing to self-evaluate, seek feedback, and continually refine their instructional approaches in alignment with best practices and student needs (Swank & Houseknecht, 2019). Building upon insights gathered during class debriefings, educators can assess the impact of creative activities after the course concludes. Evaluating teaching effectiveness, particularly in the use of creative and experiential strategies, ensures that learning outcomes are being met and that instruction remains aligned with both accreditation standards and student needs. As Nelson et al. (2020) emphasize, systematic evaluation of teaching practices enhances intentionality and supports the ongoing development of pedagogical skills in counselor education.

There are multiple ways educators can assess the outcomes of creative teaching methods. One common strategy is to distribute end-of-course surveys that include specific questions about creative activities. These surveys can ask students whether the activities supported the overall learning objectives, deepened their engagement, or helped them apply course concepts in meaningful ways. Reflective tasks, such as anonymous written feedback or digital journaling, also provide qualitative insights into how students perceived and benefited from these approaches (Lambie et al., 2018). Voluntary focus groups conducted after the course can offer more nuanced feedback and foster dialogue about students' experiences, giving voice to what worked well and what might be improved.

Educators can also assess effectiveness by analyzing grade trends, participation, and skill or knowledge acquisition growth. Using pre- and post-activity assessments allows educators to measure shifts in student learning over time. These assessments may include quizzes, performance rubrics, or reflective writing scored with evaluative criteria aligned to learning objectives.

In addition to student feedback and performance data, peer review and faculty collaboration serve as valuable tools for evaluation. Inviting a colleague to observe a class session can offer an external perspective on instructional delivery, classroom dynamics, and student engagement. Constructive peer feedback can highlight strengths and provide suggestions for improving the integration of creativity and rigor. Furthermore, sharing teaching activities and reflections with faculty who teach similar courses can promote collaboration and the exchange of ideas. Faculty learning communities and curriculum teams are excellent platforms for discussing the implementation and outcomes of innovative teaching strategies (Thacker & Huber, 2021). These collegial conversations foster a culture of reflective practice and support the collective enhancement of counselor education.

Conclusion

Cultivating creativity in counselor education is not about being artistic or inventive in the traditional sense—it's about being intentional, responsive, and bold enough to transform how we engage with students, content, and the learning process itself. Throughout this chapter, we've explored how creativity can function as more than an enhancement to pedagogy—it can serve as a guiding framework that aligns with adult learning principles (Knowles, 1968), counselor identity development (Duffy et al., 2020), accreditation standards (CACREP, 2016), and inclusive teaching practices grounded in frameworks such as Universal Design for Learning (CAST, 2024; Bills, 2021; Wilde & Banik, 2025).

Creativity invites counselor educators to move beyond rigid structures and traditional lecture formats to create classrooms that reflect the richness, complexity, and human-centered nature of counseling itself. As demonstrated through activities like the Theory Sale or identity exploration reflections, creative teaching provides space for students to think critically, engage reflectively, and integrate personal experiences into their professional growth (Lawrence et al., 2015; Coaston & Lawrence,

2019). It honors the diversity of learners by incorporating multiple modalities, scaffolding strategies, and UDL principles (McAuliffe & Eriksen, 2019; Field et al., 2022). Creativity also enables educators to adapt their approaches across developmental levels, ensuring that both foundational and advanced students are challenged and supported in meaningful ways (Storlie et al., 2015).

Importantly, creativity does not exist in opposition to structure or rigor. Instead, it thrives when grounded in thoughtful planning, clear learning outcomes, and alignment with CACREP standards and program goals (Minton & Pease-Carter, 2011; Lawrence et al., 2015). The integration of reflection, debriefing, and intentional evaluation further ensures that creativity is not arbitrary, but purposeful—enhancing students' understanding, skills, and confidence as emerging counselors (Nelson et al., 2020; Lambie et al., 2018; Rothwell, 2024).

As you continue your journey through the remainder of this book and beyond, revisit your own reflections on what it means to be a creative counselor educator. Whether you're just beginning to explore creative strategies or already implementing them with confidence, allow yourself to remain curious, flexible, and open to the process of growth. Creativity is not a one-time endeavor; it's a professional disposition—a way of seeing the world, responding to students' needs, and teaching with heart, purpose, and innovation (Lin, 2011; McGhee et al., 2019).

Counselor education is a dynamic, human field—so let us teach in ways that reflect that truth. By fostering creativity in ourselves and our students, we are not only improving classroom experiences—we are shaping a generation of counselors who can think flexibly, act ethically, and work compassionately in an ever-changing world.

Activities to Enhance Exploration

1. Journaling: After reading through the content, jump back to the five-minute written reflection from the start of the chapter and add your thoughts. Seek out a colleague or peer to discuss these reflections. This does not have to be another counselor educator. In fact, you may gain a better perspective or novel ideas from someone outside of the field and at various educational levels.

It is essential to continue this reflection by setting aside time each week to review our practices. If we do not schedule the time, priorities like reflection can easily be overlooked.

Here are a few questions to get you started:

In what ways do my current lesson plans incorporate creative elements?

How do I create an environment that encourages students to take creative risks in their learning?

How am I modeling creativity in my teaching, and how does it influence my students' approach to learning and problem-solving?

How am I ensuring that creativity in my lesson plans aligns with the learning objectives?

2. Schedule time for personal creative exploration. Set aside time outside your teaching duties to explore creative activities that inspire you. This could include pursuing hobbies, engaging in artistic endeavors, or simply trying new things that foster creativity.

3. Look to attend creative retreats and conferences. Also, explore disciplines outside teaching or counseling, such as art, theater, or design, to gather fresh perspectives and ideas.

4. Consider adding a statement to the personal philosophy of teaching that explains why creativity is essential to your work. Reflect on how you plan to integrate creative approaches into your teaching to facilitate student learning and professional growth.

5. Collaborative Lesson Planning: We often use this strategy: partner with one or more colleagues to create or revise lesson plans. By sharing ideas and reflecting on the outcomes, you can improve your work and build a culture of embracing creativity, risk-taking, and flexibility. Building this support network allows you to engage in problem-solving, brainstorming, resource-sharing, and discussing successes and challenges. For the educator, this time can be one of connection, understanding, and validation.

References

Bills, K. L. (2021). Implementing universal design for learning in higher education. *International Journal of Innovation, Creativity, and Change, 15*(3), 321–331. https://www.ijicc.net/images/Vol_15/Iss_3/15327_Bills_2021_E_R.pdf

Center for Applied Special Technology (CAST). (2024). UDL guidelines. https://udlguidelines.cast.org/

Coaston, S. C., & Lawrence, C. (2019). Integrating self-compassion across the counselor education curriculum. *Journal of Creativity in Mental Health, 14*(3), 292–305. https://10.1080/15401383.2019.1610536

Council for Accreditation of Counseling and Related Educational Programs. (2016). 2016 CACREP standards. http://www.cacrep.org/for-programs/2016-cacrep-standards/

Duffy, J. T., Springer, S., Delaney, M., & Luke, M. (2020). Eco-education: Integrating nature into counselor education. *Journal of Creativity in Mental Health, 15*(1), 55–68. https://10.1080/15401383.2019.1640152

Field, T. A., Jones, L. K., & Maxwell, K. (2022). Developmentally appropriate supervision strategies in beginning clinical courses. *Counselor Education and Supervision, 61*(3), 183–197. https://doi.org/10.1002/ceas.12255

Gladding, S. T., & Robert Casares, D. (2022). The ABCs of teaching family counseling: Putting "fun" into the fundamentals of the profession. *The Family Journal (Alexandria, Va), 30*(3), 257–260. https://10.1177/10664807211040838

Halbur, D. A., & Halbur, K. V. (2015). *Developing your theoretical orientation in counseling and psychotherapy* (3rd ed.). Pearson Education.

Hall, D. P., Waalkes, P. L., & Smith, P. H. (2021). A content analysis of counselor educators' teaching philosophy statements. *Journal of Counselor Preparation and Supervision, 14*(1), Article 3. https://research.library.kutztown.edu/jcps/vol14/iss1/3

Kearns, K. D., & Sullivan, C. S. (2011). Resources and practices to help graduate students and postdoctoral fellows write statements of teaching philosophy. *Advances in Physiology Education, 35*, 136–145. https://doi.org/10.1152/advan.00123.2010

Knowles, M. S. (1968). Andragogy, not pedagogy. *Adult Leadership, 16*, 350–352.

Lambie, G. W., Sias, S. M., Davis, K. M., Lawson, G., & Akos, P. (2018). Development of the counselor supervision evaluation rubric. *Counselor Education and Supervision, 57*(2), 86–100. https://doi.org/10.1002/ceas.12097

Lawrence, C., Foster, V. A., & Tieso, C. L. (2015). Creating creative clinicians: Incorporating creativity into counselor education. *Journal of Creativity in Mental Health, 10*(2), 166180. https://10.1080/15401383.2014.963188

Lin, Y. S. (2011). Fostering creativity through education: A conceptual framework of creative pedagogy. *Creative Education, 2*(3), 149–155. https://doi.org/10.4236/ce.2011.23021

Malott, K. M., Hall, K. H., Sheely-Moore, A., Krell, M. M., & Cardaciotto, L. (2014). Evidence-based teaching in higher education: Application to counselor education. *Counselor Education and Supervision, 53*(4), 294–305. https://doi.org/10.1002/j.1556-6978.2014.00064.x

McAuliffe, G., & Eriksen, K. (2019). *Handbook of counselor preparation: Constructivist, developmental, and experiential approaches.* SAGE Publications.

McGhee, C., Baltrinic, E. R., Laux, J., Clark, M., Liu, Y., & Harmening, D. (2019). A phenomenological investigation of creative teaching in counselor education. *Counselor Education and Supervision, 58*(2), 127–140. https://10.1002/ceas.12136

Medina, M. S., & Draugalis, J. R. (2013). Writing a teaching philosophy: An evidence-based approach. *American Journal of Health-System Pharmacy, 70*, 191–193. https://doi.org/10.2146/ajhp120418

Milgram, R. M., & Davidovich, N. (2010). Creative thinking and lecturer effectiveness in higher education. *The International Journal of Creativity & Problem Solving, 20*(1), 7–14.

Milton, C. A. B., & Pease-Carter, C. (2011). The status of crisis preparation in counselor education: A national study and content analysis. *Journal of Professional Counseling: Practice, Theory & Research, 38*(2), 5–17. https://doi.org/10.1080/15566382.2011.12033868

Moe, J., Pope, A., Dominguez, V., & Kemer, G. (2022). The influence of teaching philosophy on coverage of LGBTQ issues in counseling courses. *Counselor Education and Supervision, 61*(4), 322–334. https://doi.org/10.1002/ceas.12247

Nelson, K. W., DeWine, D. B., & Cox, J. A. (2020). The role of pedagogical training and reflective practice in counselor educator development. *Teaching and Supervision in Counseling, 2*(1), 1–12. https://doi.org/10.7290/tsc020101

Rothwell, W. J., Zaballero, A., Sadique, F., & Bakhshandeh, B. (2024). *Revolutionizing the online learning journey: 1,500 ways to increase engagement.* CRC Press.

Storlie, C. A., Parker-Wright, M., & Woo, H. (2015). Multicultural leadership development: A qualitative analysis of emerging leaders in counselor education. *Journal of Counselor Leadership and Advocacy, 2*(2), 154–169. https://doi.org/10.1080/2326716X.2015.1054078

Swank, J. M., & Houseknecht, A. (2019). Teaching competencies in counselor education: A Delphi study. *Counselor Education and Supervision, 58*(3), 162–176. https://doi.org/10.1002/ceas.12148

Thacker, A. M., & Huber, C. H. (2021). Building a culture of collaboration in counselor education: The power of faculty learning communities. *Journal of Counselor Preparation and Supervision, 14*(2), 1–21.

West, E. M., Moate, R., Baltrinic, E. R., & Fye, H. J. (2021). Counselor educators' perspectives on helpful learning for clinical mental health counseling students. *Counselor Education and Supervision, 60*(3), 235–253. https://doi.org/10.1002/ceas.12214

Wilde, M. O., & Banik, J. M. (2025). Inclusive teaching practices using the universal design for learning framework. In D. Bates & C. Ortega (Eds.), *Innovative approaches in counselor education for students with disabilities* (pp. 77–104). IGi Global Scientific Publishing. https://doi.org/10.4018/979-8-3693-3342-6.ch004

2

THE ROLES AND FUNCTIONS OF COUNSELOR EDUCATORS ACROSS LEARNING MODALITIES

The field of education is constantly evolving, requiring approaches that actively engage students and address their diverse needs. Since 2020, counselor education programs have undergone significant restructuring to meet the shifting demands of students and faculty, largely influenced by the COVID-19 pandemic. The transition to online learning in counselor training has introduced opportunities and challenges, particularly in fostering student engagement, self-care, and community-building (Saunders & Cogburn, 2024). These shifts have required counselor educators to rethink traditional pedagogical practices and embrace more flexible, inclusive, and creative strategies.

Programs have increasingly adopted both online synchronous and asynchronous models to provide virtual platforms for lectures, supervision, and counseling skill role plays, ensuring educational continuity. Hybrid formats have gained popularity as they accommodate diverse student needs. This model integrates structured face-to-face sessions with virtual components—both synchronous and asynchronous—allowing students to engage in hands-on experiential learning while

DOI: 10.4324/9781003514718-2

benefiting from remote coursework's convenience. For example, students may attend weekend or intensive in-person sessions for skill-based training, such as counseling techniques and role-play exercises, while completing discussions, readings, and assessments online. This structure ensures students receive essential interpersonal interactions and practical experiences while accommodating varied schedules and geographical constraints.

The hybrid model offers numerous advantages, particularly in counselor education, where both theoretical knowledge and practical skills are equally critical. A key benefit is the opportunity for synchronous learning, where students can practice counseling skills in real time, receive immediate instructor feedback, and engage in collaborative group work. This hands-on training is crucial for developing active listening, empathy, and ethical decision-making competencies. Meanwhile, asynchronous components provide flexibility, allowing students to access lectures, complete assignments, and participate in reflective activities independently. This self-directed aspect of learning is particularly beneficial for nontraditional students balancing work or family responsibilities and for programs seeking to reach diverse student populations.

As counselor education continues to grow and adapt to changing environments, both programs and educators must rethink their teaching and student engagement approaches. A common concern about online education is that it can feel isolating, leaving students disconnected from instructors, peers, and the learning process. However, intentional course design and facilitation strategies can effectively bridge this gap, fostering engagement and meaningful learning experiences (Benshoff & Gibbons, 2011). Research highlights the importance of social and instructional presence in online counselor education, which contributes to students' sense of belonging and academic confidence.

To support student success, counselor educators must adopt multiple roles that enhance both learning and engagement. These roles include content designer, facilitator, community builder, assessment developer, and technical manager. By thoughtfully integrating these responsibilities, educators can create a dynamic and supportive learning environment where students feel connected, engaged, and well-prepared for their professional development.

Many of the activities in this book were originally designed for in-person settings. However, the growing demand for creative approaches in online education highlights the need for adaptation. To support this shift, each activity includes a dedicated section with strategies for online implementation. These adaptations serve as starting points, encouraging educators to expand their creativity and explore new possibilities in virtual learning environments. As creative pedagogy becomes an increasingly vital component of counselor education, educators must balance structure with flexibility, innovation with intentionality, and content mastery with connection (Gladding & Casares, 2022).

Counselor Educators as Content Designers

In any learning environment—in-person, hybrid, or fully online—counselor educators often adopt the role of content designers, curating instructional materials and experiences that support student engagement, critical thinking, and professional growth. Counselor educators benefit from grounding instructional design in adult learning theory, evidence-based teaching practices, and pedagogical models relevant to graduate education (Swank & Houseknecht, 2019).

In asynchronous online courses, content design might include pre-recorded video lectures with embedded reflection questions, interactive case-based learning modules, and discussion prompts encouraging deeper exploration of key concepts such as ethics, identity development, or multicultural awareness. Emerging technologies like AI-generated role-play simulations can offer experiential learning opportunities that promote applied skills and ethical decision-making (Hall et al., 2021). These materials are crafted to capture students' attention while facilitating a more profound understanding of course content. Many of the activities listed in this book add recommendations for the asynchronous learning environment, such as providing a video covering an activity or concept to the course and then processing it through a discussion board using pictures or video.

In in-person classrooms, content design can emphasize physical engagement and collaborative learning through role plays, expressive arts activities, peer feedback sessions, or small-group projects. However, many in-person activities can be enriched through digital supplements that support continued engagement beyond the classroom. Effective content design includes balancing factual content with opportunities for reflection and application, aligning learning activities with clearly articulated goals and outcomes (Swank & Houseknecht, 2019). For example, students might prepare for an in-class discussion by watching a video or exploring a case online, then use their class time for application, reflection, and integration. This book provides a wealth of ideas for educators to utilize within their courses.

These strategies can be expanded to include real-time interaction in hybrid or synchronous online formats. For example, a live class session might begin with a short lecture or video clip, followed by small-group breakout discussions or digital collaboration tools. Educators can reinforce content across modalities by including visual aids, opportunities for verbal processing, written reflections, and hands-on demonstrations. Hybrid models are especially well-suited to combining the flexibility of asynchronous work (e.g., watching a video or reading a case study before class) with the dynamic interaction of live experiential learning during synchronous sessions.

Successful hybrid learning requires intentional planning. Instructors must structure content for maximum engagement and retention within limited timeframes, carefully prioritizing material and designing activities that build upon one another. One effective strategy is incorporating a course-wide theme, which provides continuity and enhances engagement. For example, themes such as Self-Compassion, Summer Camp, or concepts inspired by popular culture can create a cohesive learning experience, allowing students to progressively engage with ideas while maintaining a sense of curiosity and excitement. These themes also help instructors stay engaged and innovative in their teaching, encouraging them to think creatively about how to meet learning objectives.

An example of cross-modality and cross-format design appears in a sand tray-based activity included in this book, which encourages self-reflection through symbolic expression. In an in-person class, students might create physical sand trays and engage in guided processing with a partner or small group. The activity can be adapted in an online or hybrid context using a collaborative digital platform that supports multimedia input or a learning management system discussion board. Students can post images, short videos, relevant articles, or personal reflections in response to the prompt. The resulting virtual bulletin board becomes a shared creative space where students build a growing resource for understanding the therapeutic use of sand trays. This flexible approach allows the activity to remain experiential and reflective, regardless of the delivery format.

Facilitator of Learning

In all learning environments—in-person, hybrid, and online—counselor educators serve a vital role as facilitators of learning. This role goes beyond delivering content; it involves guiding, supporting, and challenging students as they engage in both structured and self-directed learning. High-quality facilitation involves varied, interactive instructional methods that engage learners across modalities, such as discussions, simulations, and case-based learning (Swank & Houseknecht, 2019).

In asynchronous settings, educators facilitate learning by establishing a consistent structure and providing clear expectations. Counselor educators teaching fully online courses may need to intentionally design for engagement, incorporating strategies to increase interaction and emotional investment (Merlin-Knoblich et al., 2022). This might include a weekly roadmap outlining learning objectives, required readings, assignments, and due dates (Greene & Poole, 2020). Educators can use visually appealing tools such as infographics, video announcements, or digital posters to enhance clarity and engagement. A recurring weekly newsletter or announcement can help students stay on track while highlighting key concepts, reminders, and encouragement.

In synchronous online environments, the facilitator manages real-time interaction using video conferencing platforms. Educators can use tools like live slide presentations, polls, and digital whiteboards to encourage student participation. For instance, polls can check comprehension of diagnostic frameworks, while shared whiteboards can support collaborative case conceptualization. Educators promote active learning through breakout groups, live role plays, and structured discussions that mirror in-person interactions. These activities allow students to apply counseling skills in real time while receiving immediate feedback and peer support.

In in-person classrooms, facilitation may include hands-on experiential learning, group discussions, and role plays embedded within the physical space. Educators can guide students through collaborative projects, use physical whiteboards or expressive arts materials, and create environments where students learn through doing. These formats are especially effective for kinesthetic learners, and they allow instructors to respond to student needs and adjust pacing in the moment.

Whether in-person, online, or hybrid, facilitation in counselor education is about cultivating connection, supporting autonomy, and promoting reflection and skill development. By embracing flexibility and creativity, educators can tailor their facilitation strategies to fit the needs of their learners while upholding the rigor and relational depth essential to the counseling profession.

Reflective Practitioner

In addition to facilitating learning, counselor educators serve as professional role models, demonstrating the core values and skills of the counseling profession—such as empathy, active listening, ethical decision-making, and cultural humility (Swank & Houseknecht, 2019). Regardless of the learning environment, modeling these competencies helps students internalize what counselors do and how they show up in relationships with clients. These intentional efforts not only promote skill development but also foster the professional identity formation that is central to counselor education.

In live sessions—whether in-person or virtual—educators can demonstrate clinical techniques through activities like modeling an intake interview, showing how to respond to a client expressing strong emotions, or illustrating culturally responsive communication. These demonstrations provide students with concrete, real-world examples of effective counseling practice. Following the modeling, students can engage in role plays or experiential exercises to practice the skills, receiving immediate, supportive feedback to help refine their approach.

Even in asynchronous settings, counselor educators can model professional behavior through pre-recorded videos, case demonstrations, or narrative examples embedded in course content. By narrating their thought process or showing video examples of counselor–client interactions, educators can still offer powerful learning moments that students can revisit and reflect on at their own pace.

Another essential teaching responsibility across learning environments is helping students navigate ethical and professional standards, particularly in evolving areas like virtual counseling and telehealth. Educators can facilitate discussions or case studies on topics such as maintaining client confidentiality during video sessions, securing digital records, or setting and maintaining professional boundaries while working from home. These conversations prepare students for the practical realities of working in remote or hybrid clinical settings and reinforce the ethical foundations of the profession.

Community Builder

Another essential role counselor educators take on is that of a community builder. Fostering a sense of connection and belonging is foundational to student success in any learning environment—whether in-person, online, or hybrid. Encouraging collaboration and peer-to-peer connection enhances student learning and mirrors the interpersonal nature of counseling work (Swank & Houseknecht, 2019).

While online education remains an important and accessible option, the findings suggest it may require more deliberate efforts to maintain student presence and interaction compared to other formats (Merlin-Knoblich et al., 2022). Educators can create inclusive virtual spaces by using structured opportunities for peer interaction, consistent instructor presence, and thoughtful facilitation of group activities. Research shows that when students feel seen and valued in online environments, their sense of community and social presence increases significantly (Benshoff & Gibbons, 2011; Li, 2024; Richardson et al., 2017). This sense of presence enhances connection and is strongly associated with higher student satisfaction and deeper engagement. In fact, Li (2024) found that social presence accounted for nearly half of the variance in satisfaction among counselor trainees, with peer interaction playing a key role in strengthening that presence.

In synchronous online courses, tools like breakout rooms can effectively promote small-group collaboration. Activities such as case study analysis, collaborative treatment planning, and guided reflections give students the opportunity to learn from one another, develop trust, and engage in meaningful dialogue. Structured peer-to-peer sharing fosters both academic growth and interpersonal connection. The activities presented in this book provide many examples of how this can be facilitated.

In hybrid learning environments, where students may only interact face-to-face periodically, building a strong sense of cohesion during those in-person sessions is especially important. Educators must intentionally create safe, welcoming spaces where students can quickly form relationships. Creative, experiential activities—such as expressive arts, group challenges, or storytelling—can help students connect deeply and quickly. Pairing these high-contact experiences with ongoing online collaboration allows the group dynamic to continue growing between sessions.

Even in traditional in-person classrooms, the community does not form automatically. Educators must intentionally structure peer interaction, group work, and open dialogue opportunities. Group norms, inclusive language, and active facilitation can help ensure every student feels valued and heard.

Assessment and Feedback

Educators are responsible for implementing fair and transparent evaluation practices and for using multiple forms of feedback to improve both teaching and learning outcomes (Swank & Houseknecht, 2019). In every learning environment—whether in-person, hybrid, or online—educators must design assessments that not only measure content knowledge but also evaluate students' ability to apply counseling concepts in real-world contexts. Thoughtfully constructed assessments ensure that learning objectives are being met and provide meaningful opportunities for students to demonstrate growth, regardless of the instructional format (Swank & Houseknecht, 2019).

Across all modalities, another critical aspect of the facilitator role is providing constructive, personalized feedback. In asynchronous and hybrid settings, this may involve written responses to assignments, highlighting students' strengths, and offering suggestions for growth. For example, a student's case conceptualization might be praised for its clarity while receiving guidance to improve diagnostic accuracy (Hall et al.,

2021). Educators can enhance the impact of feedback by using audio or video recordings to convey tone and empathy, or by using screen capture tools to visually walk through graded work.

Creative approaches to feedback can also boost engagement. For instance, gamifying progress—such as awarding milestone badges or using visual progress maps—can help motivate learners and provide a sense of accomplishment. Annotated rubrics and multimedia feedback tools offer learners accessible, actionable information that supports academic and professional growth.

In addition to evaluating academic knowledge and skills, counselor educators must also assess students' professional dispositions. Empathic and developmentally attuned communication—especially when addressing areas of concern—can help students reflect on their growth areas while maintaining trust in the educator-student relationship (Luke & Rogers, 2024). Incorporating reflective assignments and follow-up conversations can foster greater insight and receptivity, particularly when feedback touches on sensitive topics like professionalism, interpersonal effectiveness, or self-awareness.

Across modalities, assessment strategies can include scenario-based quizzes to evaluate clinical reasoning, reflective journaling to assess personal insight and self-awareness, and portfolio projects to showcase the integration of theory, skills, and ethical decision-making. In asynchronous and hybrid environments where real-time interaction may be limited, these types of assignments offer flexible yet rigorous ways to measure student competencies. In synchronous and in-person settings, educators may also incorporate live demonstrations, group presentations, or in-class simulations to assess interpersonal and counseling skills in real time.

Well-designed assessments do more than evaluate performance—they reinforce learning by encouraging reflection, synthesis, and application. Whether using rubrics to clarify expectations, offering timely and personalized feedback, or integrating opportunities for self-assessment, counselor educators play a critical role in ensuring that evaluation practices support academic achievement, personal development, and professional identity formation. By combining structure with creativity and empathy, assessment becomes a tool not just for measurement, but for transformation.

Technical Guide

Counselor educators also serve as technical guides, especially as the use of digital tools becomes increasingly integrated into teaching across all learning formats. Being prepared to navigate and troubleshoot educational technologies is an essential competency, particularly in online and hybrid environments. This includes the ability to manage learning platforms, integrate multimedia tools, and adapt to tech-related challenges in real time (Swank & Houseknecht, 2019).

In synchronous online environments, many traditional in-person activities can be adapted effectively, but doing so often requires advanced planning and contingency strategies. Technical challenges such as connectivity issues, audio failures, or problems with breakout rooms are common and require real-time problem-solving. For example, if a student is unable to access a breakout room, the instructor may need to reorganize groups, shift to a whole-class discussion, or provide an alternative task. Rather than being discouraged by these challenges, educators can view them as opportunities to model adaptability and problem-solving, which are valuable professional skills in counseling practice as well.

In hybrid learning environments, especially those involving intensive formats or weekend residencies, technical readiness and adaptability are equally important. Students may experience fatigue from long sessions, varying degrees of tech fluency, or limited access to resources. Educators should remain responsive to the energy of the group, adjusting the pacing, format, or depth of content to maintain engagement and promote meaningful learning. Integrating digital tools—such as collaborative online documents, polling apps, or visual collaboration boards—can help balance information delivery with interaction and creativity.

Even in fully in-person settings, technology can play a supportive role in enhancing instruction, from using slide decks and video demonstrations to incorporating digital platforms for collaborative reflection. However, unexpected issues can still arise, such as equipment malfunctions or inaccessible files. In all formats, the educator's role includes planning for flexibility, remaining calm under pressure, and being ready to pivot as needed to meet students where they are.

Ultimately, being a technical guide is not about mastering every platform, but about being prepared, resourceful, and student-focused. By approaching technology with curiosity and adaptability, counselor educators can create learning environments that are engaging, resilient, and responsive to the needs of today's diverse students.

Conclusion

As counselor education continues to evolve, the ability to teach creatively and flexibly across in-person, hybrid, and online environments has become beneficial and essential. The shift in educational delivery since 2020 has underscored the need for approaches that center student engagement, accessibility, and professional development while also honoring the deeply relational nature of counseling. In response, counselor educators have taken on multifaceted roles: as content designers, facilitators, community builders, assessment developers, reflective practitioners, and technical guides. Each role plays a vital part in shaping learning experiences that are not only pedagogically sound but also humanizing, inclusive, and grounded in counselor identity.

Whether adapting a sand tray activity for a digital bulletin board, fostering peer connection through breakout rooms, or navigating unexpected technology challenges during a weekend residency, counselor educators are continuously called to balance structure with creativity and flexibility with intentionality. By understanding and applying these educator roles across diverse learning environments, instructors can meet the varied needs of their students while promoting the critical thinking, self-awareness, and ethical foundations necessary for future counselors.

This chapter offers a framework for integrating creative pedagogy into counselor education and adaptable strategies for bringing traditionally in-person activities into online or hybrid spaces. The ideas and practices included here serve as a starting point—a springboard for innovation. As the field continues to grow and shift, counselor educators are uniquely positioned to lead with creativity, courage, and care. By doing so, they not only foster student success but also model the flexibility, empathy, and professional integrity that define the counseling profession itself.

References

Benshoff, J. M., & Gibbons, M. M. (2011). Bringing life to e-learning: Incorporating a synchronous approach to online teaching in counselor education. *The Professional Counselor, 1*, 21–28. https://doi.org/10.15241/jmb.1.1.21

Gladding, S. T., & Robert Casares, D. (2022). The ABCs of teaching family counseling: Putting "fun" into the fundamentals of the profession. *The Family Journal (Alexandria, Va)*, *30*(3), 257–260. https://doi.org/10.1177/10664807211040838

Greene, J. A., & Poole, T. M. (2020). Designing effective self-paced instructional materials for counselor education. *Journal of Counselor Preparation and Supervision*, *13*(3), 1–20.

Hall, D. P., Waalkes, P. L., & Smith, P. H. (2021). A content analysis of counselor educators' teaching philosophy statements. *Journal of Counselor Preparation and Supervision*, *14*(1), Article 3. Retrieved from https://research.library.kutztown.edu/jcps/vol14/iss1/3

Li, D. (2024). Social Presence as a Full Mediator between Online Interaction and Satisfaction: A Structural Equation Modeling Approach. *Journal of Educators Online*, *21*(4), n4.

Luke, M., & Rogers, J. L. (2024). The feedback paradox: Relational approaches to assessing dispositions in counselor education. *Counselor Education and Supervision*, *63*(1), 52–67. https://doi.org/10.1002/ceas.12345

Merlin-Knoblich, C., Chase, L., Smith, J. D., & Opiola, K. K. (2022). A comparison of student engagement in flipped, active lecture, and online counseling courses. *Journal of Creativity in Mental Health*, *17*(1), 27–40. https://doi.org/10.1080/15401383.2020.1822245

Richardson, J. C., Maeda, Y., Lv, J., & Caskurlu, S. (2017). Social presence in relation to students' satisfaction and learning in the online environment: A meta-analysis. *Computers in Human Behavior*, *71*, 402–417. https://doi.org/10.1016/j.chb.2017.02.001

Saunders, R., & Cogburn, B. (2024). Creativity in the online classroom: Fostering student connectedness in counselor education courses. *Journal of Creativity in Mental Health*, *20*, 1–13. https://doi.org/10.1080/15401383.2024.2375522

Swank, J. M., & Houseknecht, A. (2019). Teaching competencies in counselor education: A Delphi study. *Counselor Education and Supervision*, *58*(3), 162–176. https://doi.org/10.1002/ceas.12148

3

IGNITE YOUR PASSION
OVERCOMING BARRIERS TO CREATIVITY

Overcoming Barriers to Creativity in Counselor Education

While creativity is widely recognized as a core value in counseling, its application within counselor education is often met with hesitation, resistance, or misunderstanding. Many educators, particularly those new to the field, struggle with institutional norms, limited training, and internal barriers that inhibit the adoption of creative teaching strategies (Waalkes et al., 2022). Common misconceptions equate creativity with theatrical or artistic flair, causing some to believe they must possess innate artistic talent or develop elaborate, unconventional lessons to be considered innovative (Rinkevich, 2011; Wisdom, 2006). Others may worry that creative approaches lack the academic rigor necessary for serious learning environments. These misconceptions, combined with structural constraints such as heavy workloads, standardized assessment requirements, and a lack of professional development opportunities, make it difficult for creativity to flourish in counselor education programs (Bruneau & Pehrsson, 2014; CACREP, 2016; Livingston, 2010). Yet, creativity is not only compatible with effective counselor training—it is essential.

DOI: 10.4324/9781003514718-3

When embraced, it fosters engagement, supports reflective practice, and serves as a powerful buffer against burnout (Wells & Dickens, 2020; DeDiego et al., 2023). This chapter explores the internal and external barriers counselor educators face in embracing creativity, highlights the transformative potential of creative pedagogy, and underscores creativity's role in enhancing educator well-being, student development, and professional sustainability.

This chapter explores the role of creativity in counselor education, emphasizing its potential not only to enhance teaching effectiveness but also to serve as a preventive factor against burnout. The discussion begins by addressing the common misconceptions and systemic barriers that often discourage creative teaching practices. Many counselor educators face a lack of training, institutional support, or time to engage in innovative lesson planning. Misunderstandings—such as the belief that creativity requires dramatic flair or undermines academic rigor—can lead to hesitation, especially when combined with the demands of balancing teaching, research, service, and accreditation requirements (McCarthy, 2017; Waalkes et al., 2022; Bruneau & Pehrsson, 2014). Without adequate resources or encouragement, even well-intentioned educators may default to traditional, lecture-based methods that feel safer but may lack the dynamic engagement needed for transformative learning.

The chapter then considers how creativity is closely tied to vulnerability, authenticity, and reflective practice. Educators—particularly those early in their careers—may struggle with imposter syndrome, perfectionism, or the fear of failure, all of which can hinder creative risk-taking (Wells & Dickens, 2020; Sakulku & Alexander, 2011). However, creativity offers a path toward personal and professional growth by inviting both instructors and students to engage with openness and curiosity. Drawing on wellness models like the Indivisible Self (Myers & Sweeney, 2005) and the concept of compassion satisfaction (DeDiego et al., 2023), the chapter highlights how creative engagement can sustain energy, foster connection, and restore meaning in the educator role. The chapter concludes by advocating for a broader culture of creativity within counselor education—one that values innovation, supports risk-taking, and prioritizes educator well-being alongside student learning.

As you move through this chapter, consider the following questions:

- What assumptions or fears do you hold about creativity in your own teaching?
- When have you felt most energized or inspired as an educator? What role did creativity play in that experience?
- How do institutional expectations or cultural norms within your program support—or limit—your ability to teach creatively?
- What small changes could you make to introduce more creativity into your teaching, even within existing constraints?

These questions are designed to help you connect personally with the material and begin envisioning how creative practices can enhance both your well-being and your effectiveness as an educator.

Lack of Resources and Support

Resistance to integrating creativity in counselor education often stems from several misconceptions and structural barriers. Creativity is frequently misunderstood as requiring flashy, dramatic, or eccentric delivery, leading some to assume that engaging lessons must be theatrical or heavily reliant on artistic skill. Educators may believe they must be naturally creative or develop elaborate, hands-on activities to be seen as innovative. In addition, creative strategies are often perceived as lacking structure or academic rigor, making them appear incompatible with the seriousness of graduate-level professional training. These beliefs can cause discomfort for students who are used to traditional lectures or standardized assessments and who may struggle with open-ended, experiential tasks that push them beyond familiar learning models.

Contributing to these challenges is the fact that many counselor educators have not received formal training in creative pedagogy and may feel unprepared to implement innovative instructional strategies (McCarthy, 2017). New faculty often enter academia with limited teaching preparation and minimal supervision or feedback on their instructional approaches, leading to uncertainty and a reliance on more conventional, teacher-centered methods (Waalkes et al., 2022). In many cases, educators default to lectures and case study analysis—not necessarily out of preference, but out of necessity and familiarity.

The findings of Suddeath, Baltrinic, and Dugger (2020) further illuminate this issue by demonstrating that teaching self-efficacy is closely tied to the quality and consistency of doctoral-level teaching preparation. Their study found that structured coursework, multiple opportunities for teaching fieldwork, and regular, high-quality supervision significantly enhance new educators' confidence in their ability to teach effectively. In particular, satisfaction with supervision emerged as the strongest predictor of teaching self-efficacy, suggesting that programs that provide thoughtful mentorship and ongoing feedback better prepare future counselor educators to adopt innovative and engaging teaching methods. When this kind of intentional preparation is lacking, educators may feel hesitant to experiment with creativity, fearing failure or criticism.

Counselor educators can benefit from interdisciplinary collaboration and build confidence in using creative methods. Engaging with colleagues in fields that emphasize creativity—such as the arts, humanities, or business—can expose educators to fresh perspectives and approaches (Lawrence et al., 2015). Participating in professional development workshops, cross-disciplinary conversations, and scholarship on creative teaching can further empower instructors to expand their pedagogical toolkit.

However, institutional culture significantly shapes whether creativity is embraced or discouraged. Educators may be reluctant to try new teaching methods if their department does not value or model creative practices (Rinkevich, 2011; Wisdom, 2006). In accredited programs, the tension between innovation and compliance can further complicate the decision to take creative risks. The flexibility in how teaching preparation is implemented, such as that offered by CACREP standards, can lead to inconsistency across programs (Suddeath et al., 2020). As a result, faculty may feel unsupported in pursuing creative strategies, particularly if those strategies are not seen as aligning with institutional or accreditation expectations.

Despite creativity being a central value in counseling itself, it is often underutilized in counselor education programs. This disconnect can leave educators feeling constrained by rigid norms and expectations.

Incorporating strategies such as arts-based assignments, experiential activities, or metaphorical exercises can revitalize the learning environment and better equip students for the nuanced demands of clinical practice (Wells & Dickens, 2020).

A lack of access to professional development focused on creative teaching remains a significant barrier. When institutions fail to support or incentivize innovation, educators often revert to traditional methods that feel more manageable and familiar (Wisdom, 2006; Livingston, 2010). Expanding training opportunities and cultivating a culture that values creative pedagogy can help break down these barriers, enabling faculty to adopt engaging, dynamic approaches that enhance student learning.

Vulnerability

Defining what it means to be an effective teacher is a challenge that counselor educators face at every stage of their professional development. This understanding can fluctuate based on the subject matter, institutional expectations, and the evolving needs of students. For novice educators especially, developmental thinking often involves a tendency toward dualistic perspectives—seeking the "right" way to teach rather than exploring and cultivating their unique professional identity (Wells & Dickens, 2020). This rigid mindset can result in a disconnection from students, course material, and the learning environment.

Striving for perfection can feel like a constant pressure, especially for early-career faculty. However, shifting the focus from flawless execution to teaching with integrity allows for greater authenticity in the classroom (Palmer, 2017). Rather than aspiring to an impossible ideal of perfection, educators who center their teaching around their values and individual strengths often develop deeper connections with their students and a more fulfilling sense of purpose.

As highlighted in the previous chapter, creativity invites both educators and students into a space of vulnerability—a necessary condition for growth. When instructors allow themselves to be open, curious, and experimental in their teaching, they model the very qualities they hope to cultivate in their students. Vulnerability fosters an evolving, collaborative learning process, where both educators and learners grow together in the dynamic space of the classroom (Palmer, 2017).

Self-doubt, imposter syndrome, and the pressure to meet high expectations are common experiences for counselor educators, particularly in the early stages of their careers. These internal struggles often inhibit creative risk-taking, as educators may worry that their ideas will fall flat or appear unprofessional (Sakulku & Alexander, 2011). The drive to appear competent and polished can lead to overly cautious teaching that prioritizes safety over innovation.

This fear of failure can become a significant barrier to creativity. Educators may default to predictable and familiar instructional methods that feel more manageable but may fail to inspire student engagement. In contrast, embracing creativity offers a path toward authentic and energized teaching. When educators shift their mindset from performance to presence—teaching from who they are rather than who they think they should be—they create space for meaningful connection and personal fulfillment (Wells & Dickens, 2020).

This process closely mirrors the developmental journey of counselors-in-training, highlighting a parallel between becoming an effective counselor and becoming an effective educator. Just as students must learn to navigate uncertainty and trust their clinical instincts, counselor educators grow by experimenting, reflecting, and adapting their teaching practices. Creative pedagogy, then, becomes a vital pathway for growth—for both teacher and learner.

Creative teaching often requires educators to step outside their comfort zones and embrace their own learning process. Many worry that new methods will not be well received or that students may disengage or resist. Students, in turn, may also struggle with creative assignments, fearing judgment or feeling anxious in nontraditional learning settings. These mutual vulnerabilities can serve as a foundation for relational learning when acknowledged and explored with intention.

By openly sharing their own uncertainties and inviting students into honest dialogue about the learning experience, educators can foster a classroom culture grounded in mutual respect, reflection, and growth. When creativity is approached as a flexible and evolving practice—rather than a fixed set of techniques—it empowers both educators and students to co-create a learning environment that is dynamic, engaging, and transformative.

Classroom Management Issues

Despite the well-documented benefits of creativity in enhancing engagement and deepening learning, many counselor educators find it difficult to integrate creative approaches into their teaching. A variety of systemic and practical factors can contribute to this reduction in creativity, limiting the potential for innovation in counselor education classrooms.

One of the most significant challenges is the ongoing need to balance multiple professional responsibilities. Counselor educators are expected to juggle teaching, research, service, supervision, advising, and administrative duties—often with limited institutional support. Early-career faculty, in particular, report feeling overwhelmed by the sheer volume of competing demands. Time management becomes a persistent struggle, and the mental bandwidth required for creative lesson planning is often in short supply (Waalkes et al., 2022). When educators are constantly shifting between tasks and working under tight deadlines, creativity—something that often requires reflection, experimentation, and energy—can be one of the first things to be sacrificed.

The institutional emphasis on standardized assessments and measurable learning outcomes also constrains creativity in the classroom. While outcome-based education models are useful for demonstrating accountability and consistency across programs, they tend to privilege rigid evaluation metrics over dynamic, process-oriented learning. Creative and experiential teaching methods—such as role plays, expressive arts, or metaphor-based assignments—may not translate easily into quantifiable outcomes, making them harder to justify in environments driven by data and documentation. This pressure to "prove" effectiveness can push educators toward more traditional instructional methods, even when they believe creative approaches would be more impactful for student learning (Bruneau & Pehrsson, 2014).

Another complicating factor is the need for counselor educators to remain vigilant in assessing students' professional dispositions. Given the importance of ethical conduct, self-awareness, and interpersonal effectiveness in counseling, educators must continuously monitor student behaviors and development. This responsibility may lead faculty to favor structured, controlled classroom environments where professionalism can be easily observed and managed. As a result, they may feel hesitant to introduce creative activities that involve ambiguity, risk-taking, or emotional vulnerability, fearing that such approaches could be misinterpreted or misunderstood in high-stakes academic settings.

Assessing creativity itself presents additional challenges. Creative work often involves subjective judgments and qualitative feedback, which may not align with institutional preferences for standardized grading rubrics. Educators may feel uncertain about how to evaluate student participation in creative assignments or worry about appearing inconsistent or biased in their grading. This ambiguity can further discourage the use of innovative teaching practices, particularly for faculty who are still building confidence in their pedagogical approach.

In many cases, practical barriers such as a lack of time, institutional resources, or administrative support can also limit creativity. Heavy workloads, underfunded programs, and limited access to teaching materials or professional development opportunities all contribute to an environment where innovation is difficult to sustain. Faculty may want to introduce more creative activities but feel constrained by course schedules, content requirements, or large class sizes. These structural limitations often leave educators defaulting to traditional, lecture-based methods that feel more manageable, even if they are less engaging for students.

Moreover, counselor education programs are frequently guided by accreditation standards and institutional policies that favor conventional forms of instruction and assessment. While these standards—such as those set forth by the Council for Accreditation of Counseling and Related Educational Programs (CACREP, 2016)—are critical for ensuring quality and consistency, they may unintentionally discourage pedagogical experimentation. Faculty may feel pressure to "stay in line" with prescribed curricular frameworks, especially when creative approaches do not clearly map onto accreditation competencies or evaluation templates.

Altogether, these factors can have a cumulative effect, dampening the motivation and capacity for counselor educators to take creative risks in their teaching. Without structural support, time, and flexibility, innovation is difficult to sustain. As a result, many educators revert to more traditional pedagogical practices that, while familiar and easier to assess, may not fully support the complex, relational, and dynamic nature of counselor training.

Creativity as a Preventative Factor for Burnout

Burnout is a persistent and well-documented challenge in counselor education. It often arises from chronic stress, emotional exhaustion, role overload, and a perceived disconnection from one's professional identity and purpose. The effects of burnout do not remain confined to the individual educator; they ripple outward, influencing students' learning experiences and ultimately impacting the quality of care those students provide to future clients. When counselor educators are burned out, their capacity to teach, mentor, and engage meaningfully with students can decline. This can result in less dynamic instruction, diminished responsiveness to students' developmental needs, and lower levels of classroom engagement and innovation.

Luke and Rogers (2024) also highlight the emotional labor involved in delivering feedback on student dispositions. Educators often grapple with balancing support and accountability, especially when students respond defensively or experience feedback as threatening. To navigate these moments, the authors recommend applying empathy across four dimensions—cognitive, affective, behavioral, and cultural. When feedback is contextualized within a relational, student-centered framework, it becomes not only evaluative but developmental, promoting both competence and self-awareness.

One of the most damaging consequences of burnout is the erosion of creativity. When faculty are overwhelmed and emotionally depleted, their ability to think flexibly and respond adaptively to the evolving needs of students is compromised. This often leads to reliance on formulaic teaching strategies—methods that feel safe but may lack the vibrancy needed to stimulate curiosity, connection, and critical thinking (Wells & Dickens, 2020). The classroom becomes stagnant, with students less inspired and less likely to develop the adaptive skills required for the counseling profession.

This disconnection is particularly acute when counselor educators feel isolated, as was often the case during the COVID-19 pandemic. Remote work environments and the loss of informal peer support networks left many faculty members feeling disconnected from colleagues and their broader professional communities. DeDiego et al. (2023) emphasize the importance of restoring opportunities for collaboration and creative problem-solving to counteract the isolation contributing to burnout. Creative engagement with peers—through team teaching, joint curriculum design, or interdisciplinary projects—can reinvigorate teaching practice and enhance faculty wellness.

Creativity as an Antidote to Routine and Emotional Fatigue

Creativity can serve as a powerful buffer against the emotional toll of counselor education. Routine, unreflective teaching is one of the hidden contributors to burnout, gradually draining an educator's enthusiasm. In contrast, creative pedagogy—particularly when it includes experiential, reflective, or expressive components—invites renewed energy and engagement. These approaches challenge educators and students alike to step into vulnerability, which, rather than being a weakness, can foster deeper learning and connection (Palmer, 2017; Wells & Dickens, 2020).

Creative methods, such as role plays, debates, expressive arts, and storytelling, are more than engaging classroom activities—they support emotional regulation, self-awareness, and personal growth for both educators and students. Wells and Dickens (2020) argue that such practices cultivate authenticity and help sustain passion for teaching. Creative engagement also aligns with the Creative Self from Myers and Sweeney's (2005) Indivisible Self model of wellness, which includes elements like emotional regulation, positive humor, and work–life balance—key protective factors against burnout.

Educators who incorporate creativity into their teaching often report higher levels of compassion satisfaction—the sense of purpose and reward that comes from helping others—which is strongly associated with lower levels of burnout (DeDiego et al., 2023). When faculty derive meaning from designing innovative lessons, witnessing student growth, or facilitating transformative learning experiences, their sense of fulfillment and resilience increases.

Empowering Educators through Creative Practice

Creativity not only supports emotional well-being but also restores a sense of agency and autonomy in the classroom. In academic environments marked by institutional pressure, standardization, and high expectations, creativity becomes a means of reclaiming joy and authenticity in teaching. Flexible assignments, interdisciplinary collaborations, and the integration of expressive elements—such as music, art, or movement—can reinvigorate stale content and reconnect educators with their passion for the field (DeDiego et al., 2023).

For counselor educators, creative practices provide a needed contrast to the emotional labor involved in supporting students through their developmental journeys. Creative teaching offers outlets for renewal, humor, and connection, allowing educators to process their own experiences and emotions. These outlets are essential when managing the heavy emotional weight that often accompanies work in counselor education.

Importantly, creative engagement also stimulates intrinsic motivation, a driving force that renews educators' energy and sense of purpose. Designing a novel classroom activity, responding to student needs in imaginative ways, or experimenting with new modalities of delivery can reignite curiosity and excitement—powerful antidotes to professional fatigue.

Reflective Practice and Creativity

To help readers explore the personal and professional benefits of creativity, the following reflection prompts invite consideration of how creative experiences have enhanced well-being and teaching:

> *Can you recall a time when you felt energized and excited about your work? What were you doing? How might you incorporate elements of that experience into your teaching practices?*
>
> *Think about a time when you approached a professional challenge in a unique or creative way. What was the outcome? How might a creative mindset help you navigate future challenges in your work?*
>
> *Consider a time when your creativity sparked enthusiasm in your students. How did their engagement impact your own motivation?*

What strategies could you use to foster more of these moments in your classroom?

These reflective moments encourage counselor educators to revisit and reclaim the elements of creativity that bring joy, meaning, and vitality to their work.

Conclusion

Despite its clear benefits, many counselor educators encounter personal and systemic barriers to integrating creativity into their teaching. Self-doubt, fear of failure, and insecurity can lead to hesitation in trying new approaches, particularly for novice educators who may feel pressure to teach the "right" way (Wells & Dickens, 2020). Without confidence or support, faculty may rely on traditional, safe methods that lack energy and engagement.

Structural and cultural barriers can further inhibit creativity. Balancing teaching with administrative responsibilities, research expectations, and standardized assessments can leave little time or energy for imaginative lesson planning (Waalkes et al., 2022). Counselor education programs are often guided by accreditation standards and institutional policies that prioritize measurable learning outcomes and conventional pedagogical methods (CACREP, 2016; Bruneau & Pehrsson, 2014). These frameworks, while essential for program quality and accountability, can unintentionally discourage innovation by limiting flexibility in how learning objectives are achieved.

Moreover, the challenge of assessing creativity in a rigorous and equitable manner presents another obstacle. Because creative activities often involve subjective evaluation and process-oriented outcomes, they may not align easily with traditional grading models or performance-based rubrics.

To make creativity a sustainable part of counselor education, institutions must intentionally support it. This includes offering professional development opportunities that focus on creative pedagogy, promoting interdisciplinary collaboration, and recognizing the value of innovation in promotion and tenure processes. Creating spaces for collective brainstorming, co-teaching, and faculty mentorship around creative methods can also foster a sense of community and reduce professional isolation (DeDiego et al., 2023).

When creativity is embraced as a shared value and a practice rather than a product, it empowers educators to build more engaging, responsive, and human-centered classrooms. It models for students the importance of curiosity, flexibility, and reflective practice—qualities that are essential for effective counseling.

References

Bruneau, L., & Pehrsson, D. E. (2014). The process of therapeutic reading: Opening doors for counselor development. *Journal of Creativity in Mental Health, 9*(3), 346–365. https://doi.org/10.1080/15401383.2014.892864

Council for Accreditation of Counseling and Related Educational Programs. (2016). 2016 CACREP standards. http://www.cacrep.org/for-programs/2016-cacrep-standards/

DeDiego, A. C., McGrath, A. M., Maurya, R. K., & Szepe, A. A. (2023). Counselor educator workload and burnout in the era of COVID-19. *Counselor Education and Supervision, 62*(4), 368–383. https://10.1002/ceas.12276

Lawrence, C., Foster, V. A., & Tieso, C. L. (2015). Creating creative clinicians: Incorporating creativity into counselor education. *Journal of Creativity in Mental Health, 10*(2), 166180. https://10.1080/15401383.2014.963188.

Livingston, L. (2010). Teaching creativity in higher education. *Arts Education Policy Review, 111*(2), 59–62.

Luke, M., & Rogers, J. L. (2024). Dispositional Feedback: Interpersonally Rich and Creative Approaches. *Journal of Creativity in Mental Health, 19*(4), 586-601.https://doi.org/10.1080/15401383.2023.2297287

McCarthy, J. (2017). Teaching creativity: A look beyond counseling. *Journal of Asia Pacific Counseling, 7*(1), 37-46. DOI: https://doi.org/10.18401/2017.7.1.4

Myers, J. E., & Sweeney, T. J. (2005). The indivisible self: An evidence-based model of wellness (reprint). *Journal of Individual Psychology, 61*(3), 234–245.

Palmer, P. J. (2017). *The courage to teach guide for reflection and renewal.* John Wiley & Sons.

Rinkevich, J. L. (2011). Creative teaching: Why it matters and where to begin. *The Clearing House: A Journal of Educational Strategies, Issues and Ideas, 84*(5), 219–223.

Sakulku, J., & Alexander, J. (2011). The impostor phenomenon. *Behavioral Science Research Institute, 6*(1), 73–92.

Suddeath, E., Baltrinic, E., & Dugger, S. (2020). The impact of teaching preparation practices on self-efficacy toward teaching. *Counselor Education and Supervision, 59*(1), 59–73. https://doi.org/10.1002/ceas.12166

Waalkes, P. L., Hall, D. P., Haugen, J. S., Swindle, P. J., & Meyer, J. J. (2022). Beginning counselor educators' experiences of growth and challenges in teaching. *Counselor Education and Supervision, 61*(2), 86–98. https://10.1002/ceas.12227

Wells, P. -C., & Dickens, K. N. (2020). Creativity in counselor education: More than case studies. *International Journal for the Advancement of Counseling, 42*(2), 191–199. https://doi.org/10.1007/s10447-019-09393-7

Wisdom, J. (2006). Developing higher education teachers to teach creatively. In N. Jackson, M. Oliver, M. Shaw, & J. Wisdom (Eds.), *Developing creativity in higher education* (pp. 183–196). Routledge.

4

CREATIVE APPROACHES TO ESSENTIAL COUNSELING SKILLS

In the next section of this book, we are excited to introduce a collection of creative activities designed to enhance the teaching environment. The authors compiled our own collection of tried-and-true activities. To broaden our creative reach, we reached out to counselor educators and invited them to submit their favorite activities for inclusion in the book. The authors assessed each activity for applicability. Those contributions have been incorporated, and the names and credentials of the contributors are listed below, along with the titles of the activities. We were genuinely inspired by the enthusiastic response and the sense of connection that emerged from this call for contributions. Our hope is that these activities will spark ongoing creativity and innovation in your teaching.

Additionally, we've adapted and included published creative activities designed for counselor education. We encourage you to read these full articles, as they provide a wealth of knowledge and inspiration and can serve as a source of support in your journey as a creative counselor educator. These will be listed in each chapter's reference section.

This chapter will focus on activities and techniques for teaching essential counseling skills. Although these activities are frequently used

 DOI: 10.4324/9781003514718-4

in skill-based courses, they can also be applied across the curriculum, including orientations, content courses, remediation, and other program-specific areas. Each activity will include a list of required materials, learning objectives, instructions, debriefing questions, and adaptations for various learning environments. You can use these activities as they are designed or adjust them to meet your needs. Draw inspiration from these to enrich your activities and enhance your classroom experience.

As noted in the guide in Chapter 1, it is essential to establish protocols for situations where students may experience discomfort or distress. It is common for students to feel uneasy when demonstrating their counseling skills. This preparation ensures a safe and supportive learning environment for all participants. Please be mindful of these protocols and incorporate them when and where appropriate.

Speed Therapy

Material needed:
An agreed-upon sound or signal, such as a bell or any other inclusive alert method

Time needed:
45–60 minutes

Learning objectives:
1. Practice and refine basic counseling skills through a quick-paced, interactive format.
2. Build confidence in basic counseling skills through quick, continued practice.

Instructions:
1. Prepare the room by arranging the space in two rows of chairs facing each other so students can easily switch partners. Set up the agreed-upon sound or signal. (5 minutes)
2. Provide an overview of the activity as a "Speed Dating" event. It is a low-stakes environment where students can easily practice and reinforce their skills with each partner. (5 minutes)
3. Have students choose seats; one row will take on the role of counselor and the opposite side the client. Choose between 3 and 5 minutes on the timer and select one specific skill to focus on. For example, students take on the role of the counselor. (3–5 minutes per pair)
4. After the timer goes off, the counselor will switch chairs and continue that round of the skill. Once all have been clients' counselors, the group will switch roles and practice the same skill. This can continue for as many rounds or skills as the instructor would like. (3–5 minutes per pair)

Debriefing questions:
1. What was it like to focus on one specific skill in each round?
2. Which skill felt most natural to you? Which was the most challenging?

3. How did it feel to give or receive only nonverbal responses?
4. How did practicing open-ended questions affect the flow of the conversation?

Adaptations for other course formats:
Use breakout rooms to pair students. Each room represents a "round," where students can focus on one skill at a time (nonverbals, reflection of feeling, etc.). Rotate pairs for each skill-focused round, either manually or randomly, to simulate the "speed" aspect of the activity.

Set up discussion threads for each skill, where one student posts as the "client," and peers respond using the designated skill for that thread (e.g., one thread for reflection of feeling, another for open-ended questions). Specify that responses must align with each round's skill focus to keep students practicing one skill at a time.

Track and Ask

Alexis Wilkerson McDonald, PhD, LPC, LCMHC, PMHC, NCC
Azra Karajic Siwiec PhD, LPC

Materials needed:
None

Time needed:
30–45 minutes

Learning objectives:
1. Practice formulating and using open-ended questions to enhance client engagement and dialogue.
2. Improve tracking skills by identifying client responses that need follow-up.
3. Recognize the limitations of closed-ended questions and their impact on the conversation flow.

Instructions:
1. Arrange chairs in a circle or semi-circle to create a comfortable and visible seating arrangement. When facilitating this activity via Zoom Meeting, use the "Follow Host" feature. Enabling this feature aligns students' video feeds with the host's (instructor's) video feed, ensuring that everyone sees the participants in the same order as displayed by the instructor. (2 minutes)
2. Explain the purpose of the exercise, emphasizing how open-ended questions promote deeper client engagement. Conduct a brief practice round to illustrate what is expected before starting the activity. This practice allows students to familiarize themselves with their roles and understand the order of the activity. (5 minutes)
3. To maintain structure, clarity, and engagement, it is essential that all participants are aware of the order of role plays, whether conducted in person or virtually. Additionally, establish a clear sequence for who goes after whom, or let participants know in advance by announcing the next speaker's name. (5 minutes)

4. Begin the dialogue by making a clinical disclosure. For example, say, "I've been feeling overwhelmed at work and am unsure how to balance my responsibilities with home life." (1 minute)

5. After stating your disclosure, choose a student to your right or left to respond as a counselor. Their task is to ask an open-ended question related to your disclosure. For example, they might ask, "What does a typical day at work look like?" (1 minute)

6. The student to the left or right (following the same direction as before) will respond as the client, adding details to the initial disclosure. For example, they might say, "I have multiple projects to complete in such a short time frame, and I feel like I can't keep up." (1 minute)

7. The next student (to the left or right) will then take their turn to respond as the counselor, aiming to ask an open-ended question. This pattern continues around the circle, with students alternating between counselor and client roles. (35 minutes)

Managing closed-ended questions:

If a student asks a closed-ended question, such as, "Do you feel stressed?" the student playing the client must respond with a closed-ended answer, such as, "Yes." Following this, the next student in line must follow up by asking an open-ended question, for example, "What aspects of your stress do you think are most challenging for you?"

Debriefing questions:
1. What did you learn about the impact of open-ended and closed-ended questions?

2. What was your experience with tracking (continuing the dialogue)?

3. What insights or challenges did you face during the activity?

4. How did it feel to ask open-ended questions? What impact did you notice it had on the client's responses?

5. Give an example of an open-ended question that you felt was particularly effective. Why do you think it worked well?

6. Reflect on a time when you had to follow up on a closed-ended response. What strategy did you use, and how did it change the flow of the conversation?

7. Did you find staying present and attentive while formulating your questions challenging? If so, how did you manage that?

8. What insights did you gain about the importance of questioning techniques in facilitating therapeutic dialogue?

"Ring the Bell" Improv Activity

Ashton Keys, MS, NCC
Emeline Eckart, PhD

Materials needed:
An agreed-upon sound or signal, such as a bell or any other inclusive alert method

Time needed:
30 minutes

Learning objectives:
1. Promote flexibility in role playing by seeing mistakes as growth opportunities.
2. Build a supportive, confident learning environment through improv and peer collaboration.
3. Begin counseling skills role plays in a low-pressure, humorous setting.

Instructions:
1. Students are divided into groups of three, with each person taking on the roles of either counselor, client, or moderator. (5 minutes)
2. Students playing the role of counselor and client will ask the class for a suggestion of an event the client is discussing in their therapeutic setting and begin a traditional role-play scenario. (5 minutes)
3. At multiple times per the moderator's discretion, they may "ring the bell," and whoever spoke last must change the last thing they said and continue with the role play based on this change. (10–15 minutes)
4. Once the role play is complete, students will switch roles, allowing everyone a turn at playing each of the three roles. (10–15 minutes)

Activity example:

> CO: Hey, what brings you in today?
> CL: I've been feeling really overwhelmed.
> CO: That sounds rough.
> *DING/SIGNAL*
> CO: That sounds frustrating.
> *DING/SIGNAL*
> CO: That doesn't sound too bad.
> *DING/SIGNAL*
> CO: That sounds like I would want to scream at the top of my lungs.
> CL: Yes! I've been getting really annoyed.
> (Continue with role play)

Debrief questions:
1. Describe your experience playing the role of "Counselor" during this activity.
2. What were some challenges you encountered while participating in this activity?
3. How did your view of the activity change based on your role?
4. Describe the experience of letting go of where you thought the conversation would go and adapting to various changes.
5. What counseling skills did you need to rely on throughout the activity?
6. Describe the role humor played throughout the activity.

Adaptations for other course formats:
This activity can be adapted for an online format. Educators can utilize breakout rooms to split students into groups during synchronous online sessions. It may be a bit more challenging to achieve the natural improvisation style in an asynchronous environment. However, there are ways to create a more spontaneous improv experience. Various apps and tools can facilitate real-time interaction. By using video collaboration platforms like Flip, students can post short videos and respond with video replies.

Another approach is to engage AI chatbots in real-time unscripted conversations, with AI serving as a moderator and inserting random prompts for students to adjust their responses. Students can then download the chat and share it on a discussion board for others to reply to.

Who's Line Is It, Anyway?
(Lawrence & Coaston, 2017)

Materials needed:
Name tags

Time needed:
3 hours for all or 20–30 per activity

Learning objectives:
1. Enhance flexibility, creativity, and responsiveness in counseling sessions through improvisation.
2. Build self-awareness and awareness of others through interactive exercises.
3. Strengthen listening, interpretation, and reframing skills for therapeutic engagement.
4. Explore connections between improv exercises and counseling concepts such as immediacy, emotional attunement, and creativity.

Instructions:
Choose one or more of the following activities to use to enhance your class.

Activity 1: Divide participants into two lines facing each other. The leader begins by saying a random word, prompting the first participant in Line A to respond with the first word or phrase that comes to mind. This continues with Line B responding in turn until all participants have responded. Repeat two to three times. (20–30 minutes)

Processing questions:

How did it feel to respond spontaneously?
What patterns or hesitations emerged during the rounds?
How does this relate to helping clients feel comfortable sharing authentically?

Activity 2: Ask for six to seven volunteers at a time. Select a "director" and several "storytellers." The director points to a storyteller to begin a narrative and shifts to others unpredictably. Each storyteller must seamlessly continue the story. (20–30 minutes)

Processing questions:

What was it like to maintain the story's flow?
How did listening fully affect your ability to participate?
How does this reflect the demands of real-time counseling dialogue?

Activity 3: Assign emotions via nametags placed on participants' backs. Participants mingle, offering clues to help others guess their emotions through verbal and nonverbal cues. (20–30 minutes)

Processing questions:

What strategies helped identify the emotions?
What role did nonverbal communication play?
How can emotional attunement enhance therapeutic work?

Activity 4: Ask for four volunteers at a time. Pair two participants as "dialogue partners" and two as "subconscious voices." While partners converse on a given topic, subconscious voices intermittently interject their partner's thoughts aloud. Partners must incorporate these "thoughts" seamlessly into the conversation. (20–30 minutes)

Processing questions:

How did hearing subconscious insights change the conversation?
What parallels can you draw to reading between the lines in counseling?
How can metacommunication enhance client understanding?

Debriefing questions:
1. What did you learn about yourself during these exercises?
2. How do creativity and improvisation relate to counseling?
3. How can you apply these skills to strengthen your therapeutic approach?

Are You Listening to Me?

Erin Watson, PhD Candidate

Materials needed:
Clock/timer

Time needed:
30 minutes

Learning objectives:
1. Enhance active listening by focusing on verbal and nonverbal cues.
2. Practice giving constructive feedback to improve communication.
3. Recognize and address biases that hinder effective listening.

Instructions:
1. Begin with a warm-up where students form a circle, and each student takes turns sharing a brief personal story while the rest actively listen without interruption. (10 minutes)
2. Activity 1—Verbal vs. Nonverbal Cues
   Divide the class into pairs within the group.
   One student will speak for two minutes about a topic of their choice while the other actively listens and takes note of verbal and nonverbal cues.
   Switch roles after 2 minutes and provide feedback on what cues were noticed. (15 minutes)
3. Activity 2—Feedback Session
   Bring the group back as a whole.
   Choose a leader to share a short message with the group.
   Each student practices active listening and provides feedback on the message content and delivery. (15 minutes)
4. Discuss as a group what active listening skills were improved during the activities. (10 minutes)

Debrief questions:

1. What is the importance of active listening as a professional counselor?
2. What is one takeaway from the active listening exercise?
3. Am I understanding and sensitive to what others are communicating?
4. What are the nonverbal cues you recognized during this activity?
5. How will you incorporate active listening in your daily interactions?
6. How do you think active listening will impact your communication with others?

Adaptations for other course formats:

This activity can be utilized in synchronous online environments using videoconferencing platforms. Students can complete activities in a large group or small group using breakout rooms. In an asynchronous setting, students can record and upload their responses, watch and reflect on peers' videos, and provide feedback on the discussion board.

Pacing Go-Round
Frank Gorritz, PhD, LPC, NCC

Materials needed:
None

Time needed:
60–90 minutes

Learning objective:
1. Enable students to practice each phase, refining both pacing and their ability to maximize session time effectively

Instructions:
1. Start by reviewing and utilizing Ivey et al. (2015) who outlined a structured model to help with pacing, including five phases: Empathic Relationship, Story and Strengths, Goals, Restory, and Action. (15 minutes)
2. Assign roles related to students based on the five phases. Specifically, students must have roles designated to them as the counselor during each of the different phases of a counseling session. Students can alternate counselor roles when working with groups of two to four students, or each student can be designated as the counselor for a specific phase if working with five or more students. The client's role can also be designated among the students involved or assumed by the counselor educator leading the activity. The client actor should remain the same throughout the five phases to maintain cohesiveness in practicing the activity, though the actors can be switched out for variety and feasibility purposes. (5 minutes)
3. Start the practice session with the student assigned to the Empathic Relationship role and their pretend client. The rest of the students involved in the activity should be instructed to observe and make notes. The session should be timed for 10 minutes to give the students time to practice their counseling skills as they begin a session and build rapport with the client. This

is also a good opportunity for the student in this role to discuss informed consent briefly and limits to confidentiality with the pretend client. Once the ten minutes are up, all students, especially the counselor, will debrief for five minutes to reflect on how engaging in the first phase of the session felt. (15 minutes)

4. The next phase of the counseling session should begin with the student assigned to the Story and Strengths role, resuming the role of the counselor as they continue their work with the pretend client. Continue with the 10-minute time limit and 5-minute debrief; continue with the rest of the phases. (45 minutes)

Debrief questions:

1. How did it feel to conduct this part of the session?
2. What are some strengths and areas for growth for you when participating in <blank role> (e.g., building rapport with clients)?
3. What are some discomforts you noticed when participating in <blank role> (e.g., asking clients questions)?
4. What are some insights that came up for you when observing your classmates practicing?
5. Which counseling skills would you like more support in developing?
6. Which phase of the session would you like more practice in?
7. What are some ways you can enhance your participation in <blank role> (e.g., setting goals with clients)?

Adaptations for other course formats:

This activity can be utilized in synchronous online environments via videoconferencing platforms. For asynchronous settings, start by providing students with recorded video lectures or narrated slide presentations that explain Ivey et al.'s (2015) five-phase model. Pair these materials with a written summary or infographic for easy access. Students should complete a brief quiz or reflection assignment to confirm their understanding of the phases before moving on to the next step. Next, assign students into groups of two to five using a discussion board. Provide clear instructions regarding role assignments for the activity, clarifying that each student will assume the role of the counselor for a specific phase or alternate roles if in smaller groups. Assign the client role to a consistent member within the group for each session or allow the group to make that decision. Students should record video or audio sessions simulating each phase of the counseling process. Other group members should review the recordings and provide feedback using a shared document or discussion thread, guided by specific debrief questions. Repeat this process for each phase, ensuring that all students have the opportunity to participate in each role.

Reference

Ivey, A. E., Ivey, M. B., & Zalaquett, C. P. (2015). *Essentials of intentional interviewing: Counseling in a multicultural world.* Cengage Learning.

Open or Closed?

Michelle Dunn, LPC, Doctoral Candidate

Materials needed:

An agreed-upon sound or signal, such as a bell or any other inclusive alert method.

List of questions identifying open-ended and closed-ended examples, as well as prompts to convert closed-ended questions into open-ended ones.

Time needed:

30 minutes

Learning objectives:

1. Accurately identify open-ended and closed-ended questions, understanding their distinct purposes in counseling to facilitate effective client interactions.
2. Practice converting closed-ended questions into open-ended ones, enhancing their ability to ask questions that encourage client exploration and deeper responses.
3. Engage in a fast-paced, team-based activity, building skills in quick, purposeful questioning while fostering a collaborative learning environment.

Instructions:

1. Split the class into two teams. One person from each team will come to the front of the buzzer or the agreed-upon signal. If online, identify who will be playing first and use the hand-raising option. (5 minutes)
2. The instructor will read a question, and the students will have to identify whether it is open-ended or closed-ended. Whoever answers correctly gains a point. If the question is closed-ended, the student can then earn an extra point by converting it into an open-ended question. An instructor can also use questions such as "Change this question to an open-ended question." (5 minutes)

3. The students will switch out, and the instructor will read a different question. Continue playing until the end of the questions. (20 minutes)

Debrief questions:
1. What was this experience/game like for you?
2. Did you find it difficult to change closed-ended questions?
3. What were the common themes among the open-ended questions?
4. What were the common themes among the closed-ended questions?
5. When would it be appropriate to ask a closed-ended question in a counseling session?
6. Why is this an important counseling skill to learn?

Adaptations to other course formats:
In an asynchronous environment, educators can design a quiz or game-based activity and share it with the class to complete independently within a designated timeframe.

Enhancing Awareness and Empathy with Mindfulness Activities

Lien Nguyen, PhD, LPC, NCC

Materials needed:
Depending on the type of mindfulness activity chosen, materials can include one or more of the following:
Coloring pages (with themes of your choice) and coloring supplies (crayons, colored pencils, etc.)
Stress balls or similar objects
Chocolate bars, candies, or snacks
A computer with internet access and speakers

Time needed:
5–15 minutes

Learning objectives:
1. Define mindfulness and its key components, including present-moment awareness and nonjudgmental acceptance.
2. Engage in a guided mindfulness activity to enhance their own attention, awareness, and emotional regulation skills.
3. Reflect on how mindfulness can be integrated into therapeutic settings and practice explaining it as a coping strategy for clients.

Instructions:
Instructors can choose one of the mindfulness activities listed below to use in the classroom for each class:

Deep breathing and mindful listening:
1. Verbally invite students to make themselves comfortable.
2. They can choose to close their eyes or keep them open, preferably focusing on a single object if their eyes are open.
3. Instruct students to take three (3) deep breaths, modeling the breathing along with them.

4. Then, invite them to relax their muscles—starting from the head and moving down through the face, neck, shoulder, back, stomach, legs, thighs, arms, hands, fingers, feet, and toes.

5. Play calm and relaxing music, nature sounds, meditation sounds, a muscle relaxation technique video, or a loving-kindness meditation of your choice (available on YouTube or other platforms) for 2–6 minutes.
   Note: Gradually increase and decrease the volume at the beginning and end to avoid sudden loud noises. Pay attention to the lighting, as excessive brightness can reduce the mindfulness effect.

6. Encourage students to fully engage in the moment, using their five senses to notice what is happening (what they see, whether on the slide or in their minds, what they hear, and what they feel). For guided imagery videos, students may follow the instructions provided.

7. Use the debrief questions below to help students process their experience, as applicable (2–3 minutes).

Mindful eating:

1. Invite students to choose a piece of the food provided (such as chocolate, snacks, or candies) according to their preference.

2. Instruct students to eat the food mindfully, focusing on the taste. While eating, encourage them to mentally answer the question, "How is the food? What do you notice?" (2–5 minutes). Note: Ask students if they have any allergies to the provided food ingredients and inform them that they do not have to eat the food if they are uncomfortable.

3. Use the debrief questions below to help students process their experience, as applicable: What did you notice/taste/smell? How do you feel now? Did you get distracted? If so, did you bring yourself back to the moment? (2–3 minutes)

Mindful coloring:

1. Provide coloring pages with themes such as positive affirmations, seasonal motifs, nature, etc., along with coloring materials.

2. Instruct students to color the pages and encourage them to enjoy the process while staying present. While coloring, they can mentally reflect on the question, "What is/are in the picture/coloring page?" (5 minutes)

3. Use the debrief questions below to help students process their experience, as applicable: What did you notice or see? How do you feel now? Did you get distracted? If so, did you bring yourself back to the moment? (2–3 minutes)

Nature walk:

1. If the weather permits, take students outside. Instruct them to select a spot on campus close to the group and the instructor where they can enjoy the weather and the moment. Encourage them to use their five senses to observe and acknowledge what is happening around them (5 minutes).

2. Return to the classroom and help students process their experience using the debrief questions below (2–3 minutes).

Gratitude:

1. Invite students to silently reflect on three things they are grateful for today (5 minutes).

2. Ask students to share, at their comfort level, what they are grateful for today (2–5 minutes).

Stress balls/similar objects:

1. Invite students to choose one object from the options provided.

2. Instruct students to examine the object by touching and squeezing it mindfully.

3. Use the debrief questions below to help students process their experience as applicable: What did you notice or see? What did you feel? How do you feel now? Did you get distracted? If so, did you bring yourself back to the moment? (2–3 minutes).

Finding differences/characters/objects in pictures:

1. Show students pictures and ask them to find differences between two images or locate a specific character, person, or object in

the picture (e.g., finding Waldo). Use more than one picture if needed (3–5 minutes).

2. Use the debrief questions below to help students process their experience as applicable: What did you notice or see? How do you feel now? Did you get distracted? If so, did you bring yourself back to the moment? (2–3 minutes)

Debrief questions:
1. What did you notice?
2. What did you see?
3. What did you hear?
4. What did you taste?
5. What did you smell?
6. What did you feel?
7. How do you feel now?
8. Did you get distracted? If so, did you bring yourself back to the moment?

Adaptations for other course formats:
Mindfulness activities can be tailored to various course formats, enabling instructors to select options that fit their specific classroom environments. In an in-person setting, all the mentioned mindfulness activities are applicable and easily implemented. For synchronous online classes, activities such as deep breathing, mindful listening, mindful coloring, practicing gratitude, or identifying differences in pictures or characters are effective. Instructors can utilize online resources, like digital coloring pages, images, and videos, to boost engagement in a virtual format. Regardless of the environment, it is crucial to encourage students to engage fully and ensure they feel comfortable using digital tools. Providing support or tutorials as needed will help foster effective participation.

Narrative: Objects of Memory

Xiaoxuan Qu, PhD

Melissa Luke, PhD, LMHC, NCC, ACS

Materials needed:

The Objects of Memory video (Young, 2017)

Time needed:

40 minutes–1 hour

Learning objectives:

1. Develop active listening skills to interpret client narratives into clinically relevant data.
2. Practice identifying and understanding the significance of the client's experiences through the stories shared about meaningful objects.
3. Enhance the ability to reflect on and generate new meanings from clients' narratives.

Instructions:

1. Play video as an in-class activity (20 minutes)
2. After watching the video, show processing questions (see below; 1–2 minutes)
3. Ask counselors-in-training to pick one or two questions to respond to (20–30 minutes)

Debrief questions:

1. How does each individual tell their stories and memories?
2. What significance does the object hold for each individual?
3. How are our memories inscribed in the objects we accumulate?
4. How do we curate our own histories and identities through the collection of memory?
5. What does the object that each individual has chosen say about them as social and cultural beings?
6. If you were asked to share an object with the class, what would you choose?

7. How would you tell your story? In what ways do your object and story speak to you as a counselor-in-training?

Adaptations for other course formats:
In addition to in-person learning, this narrative video can be played in a virtual classroom or assigned as an asynchronous assignment.

Reference

Young, P. E. (2017). *Objects of memory*. ERRATICA. https://vimeo.com/223195423

Reflecting in a Fishbowl

Mindy Heher, PhD, LPC, NCC, ACS

Materials needed:
Role-play Scenarios

Time needed:
The time needed will vary according to the number of students in the class. At a minimum, one reflecting team exercise, focused on one dyad, could be completed in 30 minutes.

Learning objectives:
1. View client issues through a systemic lens, recognizing that problems and meanings are co-constructed within relationships, enhancing their ability to think collaboratively and contextually about client concerns.
2. Improve their critical thinking and problem-solving abilities by observing, analyzing, and providing thoughtful feedback to peers in the form of "I wonder" statements, fostering intentional and reflective insights.
3. Practice delivering nonjudgmental, constructive feedback in a respectful and supportive manner, promoting a safe, non-threatening environment for self-reflection and growth as future counselors.

Instructions:
1. The instructor creates a large circle with chairs and places two chairs in the middle of the circle facing each other.
2. The instructor either creates the dyads or asks the students to pair up with one another.
3. Once the dyads are formed, the instructor provides a copy of the role-play scenarios to each dyad and allows the pairs 5–10 minutes to review the scenarios. Each student will choose a client to role-play. Dyad partners are permitted to share their chosen client with each other for their role play.

4. The instructor asks for dyads to volunteer to role-play or calls the dyads to the fishbowl.

5. The first dyad sits in the two chairs in the middle of the fishbowl and engages in their role play while their peers observe quietly in the circle around them.

6. The instructor sets a 15-minute timer for the role play.

7. At times, the reflecting team spends 10 minutes respectfully sharing their thoughts about what they heard and observed by offering feedback one at a time. The feedback provided is concise and specific in the form of statements beginning with "I wonder," followed by their thoughts. For example, "I wonder if reflecting more of the client's feelings would help the client explore their emotions more deeply." Each member of the team is allowed to share one "I wonder" statement. Therefore, they must be deliberate and thoughtful with their feedback. This not only enhances their critical thinking skills but also helps to keep time.

8. While the reflecting team offers their feedback, the therapist in the role play listens quietly and attentively and does not engage in conversation with the reflecting team or the person role playing the client. The therapist may take notes while hearing the feedback.

9. At the conclusion of the reflecting team discussion, the student role playing the client is given the opportunity to offer their feedback.

10. Once all feedback has been shared by the reflecting team and client, the student role playing the counselor is given about 5 minutes to respond to any of the team's comments.

11. The exercise continues until each dyad is given the opportunity to role-play.

Debrief questions:

1. How did this activity help you understand your role as a counselor better?

2. How did your understanding of your role as a counselor change as a result of this activity?

3. How did hearing the "I wonder" statements from your peers impact your understanding of the client?

4. How do you think this activity will influence your approach to counseling in the future?

5. How did this activity help you understand the perspectives and experiences of your client?

6. What aspects of your approach or counseling skills would you like to improve based on your peers' statements?

7. How can you use the insights gained from this role play to better prepare for real counseling situations?

8. Were there any aspects of the role-play scenario that you found particularly helpful or challenging?

Adaptations for other course formats:
Implementing the reflecting teams in fishbowls activity in an asynchronous format is achievable. In this online discussion board activity, students collaborate in dyads to create a role-play video recording and post the link to the video on the course discussion board. Over the course of a week, classmates review the video and provide "I wonder" feedback statements as replies to the counselor's post. At the end of the week, after reviewing the feedback, the counselor synthesizes it and shares a reflective response guided by the activity's debrief questions.

Broaching with Figures

Materials needed:
A set of diverse figures (or virtual images if online), including a wide range of animals, finger puppets, or other figures.
Printed handouts or virtual images of a Venn diagram.

Time needed:
70 minutes

Learning objectives:
1. Develop skills in broaching topics around identity, culture, and personal challenges in a supportive, non-threatening way.
2. Cultivate empathy by interpreting animals as symbolic representations of diverse client identities, cultures, or struggles.
3. Reflect on their comfort levels by initiating conversations about topics that may feel sensitive or challenging.

Instructions:
1. Begin by introducing the concept of broaching and discussing its importance in establishing a therapeutic alliance, especially when working with diverse clients. Emphasize that broaching requires both empathy and sensitivity. Explain that animal figures or finger puppets will be used as symbols to help students practice broaching different identities and personal challenges indirectly, allowing them to engage with difficult topics more creatively and thoughtfully. (10 minutes)
2. Randomly pass out or assign figures or images to students. (5 minutes)
3. Place students into dyads or triads and provide each pair with a Venn diagram. Have the students identify similarities and differences between their figures. (10 minutes)
4. Using the identified similarities and differences, have the students practice the counselor, client, and observer roles. Each student will practice role playing broaching as if they were the figure they chose. (30 minutes)

5. This could be a difficult task, so check in with the class and see if they are struggling. You can provide the class with a list of broaching sentence stems to get them started:

    - "I'm interested in learning more about your cultural background. Can you share a bit about that?"
    - "What's one thing you need to feel safe and understood in your environment?"
    - "Sometimes, being an [animal] means having values that others don't understand. What are some values or priorities that guide you in your life?"
    - "There are many stereotypes about being a [animal]. Which ones bother you, and which ones do you feel truly reflect who you are?"
    - "I'm committed to creating a safe and inclusive space for our sessions. Is there anything specific about your identity or background you'd like me to be aware of or consider?"
    - "I want our counseling space to be inclusive and supportive. How can we integrate discussions about diversity into our sessions in a way that feels meaningful to you?"
    - "In the animal world, family dynamics can be very different. As an [animal], how do you relate to family or close connections?"
    - "In a world full of many different animals, how does being a [animal] impact how you interact with others? Do you ever feel like you have to change who you are?"

Debriefing questions:
1. What was it like to use an animal figure or finger puppet to broach a potentially sensitive topic?
2. How did using an animal or finger puppet change your comfort level with broaching?
3. What did you learn about your approach to broaching?
4. How can this practice inform your approach to real clients?

Adaptations for other course formats:

This activity can be utilized in synchronous online environments via videoconferencing platforms. Use slides or visuals to explain that broaching requires empathy and sensitivity and share how animal figures or images can serve as symbolic tools to help students approach sensitive topics creatively and thoughtfully.

Building Empathy through Song Exploration

Materials needed:

Headphones or speakers

Access to various songs from different genres (e.g., blues, jazz, pop, hip-hop, classical, country, folk, rock)

Printed or digital copies of song lyrics

Time needed:

45–60 minutes

Learning objectives:

1. Explore how music can convey emotions and personal experiences, allowing people to better understand and empathize with diverse perspectives.
2. Learn to distinguish between the emotions conveyed through melody and those expressed through lyrics, enhancing their emotional awareness and listening skills.
3. Practice self-reflection, examining how they respond emotionally to both music and lyrics and understanding how these reactions can shape empathetic listening.

Instructions:

1. Begin by discussing the role of music in expressing emotions and experiences, often providing a window into the lives of others. Explain that the goal of the activity is to help students connect with and empathize with diverse experiences through music. (5 minutes)
2. As a class, build a playlist of songs from various genres that depict a range of emotions or life experiences. This list can be as small or large as the class would like. This can be used as a regular activity to start or end class time or used in a weekly announcement or discussion post. (15 minutes)
3. The class will listen to each song in two stages: first, focusing on the music (melody, rhythm, tone), and then focusing on the lyrics. (5 minutes per song)

4. After each stage, discuss as a large group some of the emotional reactions, any thoughts on the mood or story suggested by the music alone, and then the lyrics. Then, reflect on how the lyrics add context or depth to the emotions and whether they change or reinforce their initial reactions. (15 minutes)

Debriefing questions:
1. What emotions did you initially feel when listening to the music alone?
2. How did the lyrics change or enhance your understanding of the song's emotion or message?
3. Were there any emotions or experiences in the lyrics that challenged you or surprised you?
4. How can this experience of interpreting emotion in music help you as a counselor?

Adaptations for other course formats:
This activity can be easily adapted to an online format using video conferencing software and sharing the songs. For an asynchronous adaptation, it can be designed to foster creativity and reflection while maintaining a flexible structure. Create a collaborative playlist on platforms like Spotify or YouTube, where students can contribute songs that represent a variety of emotions or life experiences. Post a discussion thread or shared document inviting students to add their selections to the playlist, along with a brief explanation of why they chose each song and how they believe it reflects a specific emotion or experience. This playlist can be continually updated and included in weekly announcements or discussion posts, promoting ongoing engagement. Students can listen individually and share their thoughts and reflections.

Skill Building on Rupture and Repair in the Counseling Relationship

Carrie VanMeter, PhD, LPCC, LSC
Clarissa Mulligan Attara, PhD, LPC, LMHC, LCADC, ACS, CCS, CCTP

Materials needed:
Case vignette(s)

Time needed:
1 to 2 hours, depending on the format selected

Learning objectives:
1. Identify dynamics of ruptures in the therapeutic relationship.
2. Practice advanced skills for addressing and repairing ruptures in the therapeutic relationship.
3. Engage in discussions to facilitate the repair of the therapeutic relationship.

Instructions:
1. Introduce the topic of rupture and repair in counseling to the students via a mini-lecture or discussion with the class. The instructor could also share some of the articles or YouTube examples to facilitate an educated conversation on the topic of rupture and repair in the counseling relationship. Goldsmith (2013) may be an article to share to explain rupture and repair (article referenced at the end). (20 minutes)
2. Vignette(s) are provided to the students, or they can create their own vignettes. Creating their own vignette would demonstrate a further understanding of when/how ruptures occur. If there is not enough time, the instructor can create the vignette(s). Provided below are examples that could be used. (If students are creating their own, 15 minutes)

    Vignette 1: In the first appointment, Mae comes to the initial evaluation for their first time in counseling. They are nervous as they are not sure what to expect, but excited to finally be taking this step after debating for the last two years. Mae has a history of substance use, as the counselor learns during the first few questions of the evaluation. As the counselor asks all of the questions required for the initial evaluation appointment, once Mae tells the counselor they drink four to five drinks per occasion, and they are unsure how many times a week, the counselor seemed to, from Mae's perspective, focus only on this. Mae insisted the reason they were there was to figure out how to come out to their sister and to work on some conflicts they felt due to their religious beliefs and their self-acceptance. You also overheard the counselor from the first appointment use incorrect pronouns about your client in front of your client (you know because the intake paperwork had the correct pronouns: they/them, but your colleague switched between he and she and appeared frustrated). You are Mae's counselor, and you are meeting with them for the first appointment after their initial evaluation with another counselor. They mention to you their experience.

Vignette 2: Jax comes in for his first counseling session, hopeful that his counselor will be able to help him. He has been feeling "depressed for a while," and it has taken everything in him to come to this appointment today. He shared how sad he has been and how recently his sister really hurt his feelings when she said, "the whole family is sick of you being so depressed already; I mean enough is enough!" You had a lot of questions to ask, so you did not address the emotion or validate his feelings. You quickly moved on to the next question on the list without acknowledging or addressing what was said; after all, you only have 60 minutes to get all of your questions answered and information completed. You noticed Jax was upset, but you thought, "next time I will be able to give him more time to explore his feelings; today isn't for that."

3. Depending on the class setup, students are paired or grouped to complete a role play based on the vignette. They are instructed to engage in the role play as if this is the session after the situation in the vignette. The role play should take five to 10 minutes, depending on the situation. The student playing the counselor will be expected to attempt to repair the relationship.

The student playing the role of the client will offer some realistic resistance based on the situation in the vignette to allow the counselor to work through the repair process after a rupture. Have students switch roles so everyone gets a turn to be the counselor. (20–30 minutes)

4. Instruct the pairs or small groups to debrief the experience following the activity. They can explore how the role play went, highlighting strengths and areas for growth. (10 minutes)

5. The class would return as a whole and discuss reactions and takeaways from the activities. The instructor will want to normalize the experiences, including personal issues or feelings that may have arisen for the counselor in these role plays, as these arise in counseling sessions, and highlight the importance of continued supervision and consultation. (10 minutes)

Debrief questions:

1. What was most challenging about this role play as the counselor? As the client?
2. What surprised you during this role play?
3. How do you see supervision being useful when you encounter ruptures in the counseling relationship?
4. How did the repair activity impact the counseling relationship?
5. What do you think would happen if there were no repair in this situation?
6. How can you assess if a repair is successful in a counseling relationship?

Adaptations for other course formats:

The activity is adaptable to most formats and class sizes. If completed virtually, it is recommended that break rooms be utilized. If completed asynchronously, there is the potential to record and review role plays and have the student complete a short write-up on the experience. The instructor could give feedback on the recording and insight into the write-up.

Reference

Goldsmith, J. (2013). *The value of difficult moments in the client-therapist relationship.* The Family Institute of Northwestern University. Clinical Science Insights. https://www .family-institute.org/sites/default/files/pdfs/csi_goldsmith_therapist_relations

ClientGPT: Using Generative AI for Counseling Skills Mastery

Saiber Shaikh, MA, MSEd

Materials needed:

Computer or tablet with internet access.

Access to a Generative AI program capable of creating and interacting with AI characters, such as characters.ai website.

Pre-designed client profiles/case studies/vignettes, including relevant demographic information and presenting problems.

Time needed:

2 hours

Learning objectives:

1. Develop core counseling skills through interactive simulation
2. Critically evaluate and reflect on AI-Assisted Counseling Interactions
3. Understand and practice the application of generative AI in counseling skill development

Instructions:

1. Preparation phase: The instructor creates an AI "client" character using a Generative AI platform such as character.ai or ChatGPT, inputting relevant background information such as age, gender, and presenting problem. (35 minutes)

    • Using Character.ai: Have students create a free account on Character.ai.

    • Instructors can create custom AI clients for assessment and practice, editing each "client" as needed for different interactions.

    • Set visibility to "Unlisted" so that only students with the link can access the character, keeping it private.

    • Use the "More Options" feature to add character details and specific interaction rules to enhance realism. For example, define personality traits or background information.

- Ensure the AI client doesn't ask questions by including a "no questions" rule to maintain the client-counselor interaction flow.
- Character.ai is developing group chats and voice responses, which can further enhance the activity when they are available.

2. Students are briefed on the activity and their accessibility to the website, and AI character is verified. They are also given information about the basic counseling skills they should focus on during their interaction with the AI Client (e.g., paraphrasing, reflection of feeling, open-ended questioning, empathic responding, pattern recognition, etc.). (15 minutes)

3. Students can work individually or in groups to interact with the AI client to practice their skills. If groups are used, students take turns interacting with the AI client for 5–10 minutes, practicing their counseling skills. Observing students take notes on their peers' performance.

   Students can also pause the chat and ask the GenAI to respond on how they are doing and what can be improved. (10 minutes—repeat as needed)

   They can also request alternative responses that might have been a better choice if they made a mistake or felt they could have performed better. While testing the characters.ai model, it demonstrated an understanding of the fundamental principles of therapeutic interactions and provided feedback when responses were nontherapeutic or lacked empathy. Therefore, it can function as a learning tool for basic counseling skills and building a therapeutic alliance.

4. Instruct the pairs or small groups to debrief the experience following the activity. They can explore how the interactions went, highlighting where they felt stuck and brainstorming potential improvements. (10 minutes)

5. The class would return as a whole and discuss reactions and takeaways from the activities. The instructor provides additional feedback and guidance. (20 minutes)

6. Students write a brief reflection on their experience and areas for improvement. They can attach screenshots of their transcripts to demonstrate skill application or improvement. The instructor reviews the reflections and provides individual feedback.

Debrief questions:
1. What counseling skills did you find easiest to implement? Which were the most challenging?
2. How did the AI client's responses influence your choice of interventions?
3. In what ways did this experience help you understand the importance of adapting your approach to each client's unique presentation?
4. What patterns did you notice in your own responses or tendencies during the interaction?
5. How might this experience translate to real-world counseling situations?
6. How did observing your peers' interactions impact your understanding of effective counseling techniques?
7. What surprised you most about this experience?
8. How has this activity influenced your confidence in your counseling skills?

Special considerations
Ensure that students understand the limitations of AI and that these interactions are for skill practice, not to replace human-to-human learning experiences. Address potential technical issues beforehand and have a backup plan (e.g., pre-written scripts) in case of AI platform downtime. Be prepared to discuss the ethical implications of AI in counseling and counselor education. Let students know that AI at this nascent stage can have bias in responses and can respond with information that is incorrect or harmful.

Adaptations for other course formats:
In an asynchronous format, instructors can provide pre-recorded instructions and examples of AI interactions for students to watch and learn

from. Students can then engage with the AI client independently and share their experiences on discussion boards or forums, where they can also receive feedback from peers and instructors. For a virtual synchronous setting, instructors can use breakout rooms for small group discussions, allowing students to discuss and reflect on their AI interactions in real time. Sessions can be recorded, giving students the chance to revisit the material as needed. In an in-person environment, instructors can conduct AI interactions in a computer lab, where students engage with the technology in a shared setting. Face-to-face group discussions and role plays can be facilitated to deepen learning and allow students to practice skills in both AI and human-to-human scenarios.

Reference

Character Technologies, Inc. (2024). characters.ai (September 15th, 2024 version) [Large language model]. https://character.ai/

Emotional Charades

Azra Karajic Siwiec PhD, LPC
Alexis Wilkerson McDonald, PhD, LPC, LCMHC, PMHC, NCC

Materials needed:
None

Time needed:
15–25 minutes

Learning objectives:
1. Develop an understanding of cultural diversity in facial expressions, increasing sensitivity to subtle cues that clients may display in counseling settings.
2. Practice identifying micro-expressions and interpreting various emotional cues accurately, gaining insight into how emotions are expressed differently across cultures.
3. Build self-awareness by exploring the intentional use of facial expressions, allowing them to recognize and refine their own nonverbal cues to enhance therapeutic rapport and cultural responsiveness.

Instructions:
1. Instruct the group that they will play the game of charades.
2. The main expression should be the use of your face, particularly microexpressions (small expressions that tell the person how they feel); they give insight into what they are communicating.
3. Each person will be able to communicate an emotion strictly through facial expressions.
4. One after another, people will go in the circle communicating an emotion, and each will offer their interpretation of what emotion the communicator was attempting to express.
5. After each person has had an opportunity to offer their interpretation, then the communicator will share what they hoped to have communicated to the group.

6. The communicator must then share what aspect of their face communicated what they hoped to have expressed. The communicator should address the intentionality behind the facial expression to build self-awareness. This can create a dialogue among the group about what was expressed compared to how it appeared.

Debrief questions:

1. What did you learn about the power of nonverbal communication and emotional expression?
2. What was your experience with trying to understand the expression?
3. For the communicator, what is the feature of the facial expression as well, and where did you adopt/learn it?
4. For the communicator—how did the interpretations you heard impact your self-awareness?
5. How important is emotional expression and nonverbal communication?
6. What insights or challenges did you face during the activity?
7. What bias may have occurred at any of the points, and how may it be divergent from the "first impressions" you formed of this person?

Adaptations for other course formats:

This activity can be effectively adapted for both synchronous and asynchronous online environments. In a synchronous setting, video call platforms can be utilized. The group can then discuss their interpretations, and the person expressing the emotion can clarify their intended expression. For asynchronous adaptation, students can record short video clips of themselves demonstrating a specific emotion through facial expressions only and post them to a shared discussion board. Peers would then watch these videos and comment on what they believe the emotion is, followed by the original poster revealing their intended expression and reflecting on which facial aspects they used to convey it.

Are You Prepared to Conduct a Spiritual Assessment?
Cassandra Johnson, PhD, LPC, CPCS

Materials needed:
Dr. Johnson's Brief Spirituality Assessment Questions

- Do you have a spiritual belief and if so, which belief do you identify with?
- How does spirituality play a role in your life?
- Do you have an interest in including spiritual interventions in treatment?

Time needed:
10–15 minutes

Learning objectives:
1. Identify the significance of addressing spiritual beliefs in the counseling process.
2. Practice implementing spirituality in questions into assessment.
3. Identify and reflect on how personal beliefs and spirituality may influence the counseling process.
4. Become familiar with the role of the ACA code of ethics and ASERVIC guidelines in addressing spiritual needs in counseling.

Instructions:
1. Provide a discussion surrounding the importance of addressing spiritual beliefs in the counseling process, beginning at assessment. Discuss the ACA and ASERVIC guidelines regarding addressing spiritual needs in counseling.
2. Place students into triads or dyads. Students will each take the part of counselor and client. The counselor will greet the client and explain the importance of a spiritual assessment. Then, the counselor will ask the client Dr. Johnson's Brief Spirituality Assessment Questions. Once the questions have been asked and

answered, the students can switch roles, allowing the other to practice.

This script can be utilized:

"Hi Jane! Thanks for coming in today! I would like to continue the assessment process by asking you about your spiritual preferences. Knowing this information is important in gaining a complete picture of your identity and in determining how we will work together. Is that alright with you?"

"Great! Tell me:

- Do you have a spiritual belief and if so, which belief do you identify with?
- How does spirituality play a role in your life?
- Do you have an interest in including spiritual interventions in treatment?"

3. Come back to the large class and discuss the activity.

Debrief questions:
1. How did you feel about completing this activity
2. What does your spiritual identity look like?
3. How does having self-awareness of your spiritual identity play a role in confidently assessing the spiritual identity of clients?
4. What concerns do you have about conducting a spiritual assessment?
5. Are you familiar with ASERVIC? If not, how will you ensure that you are knowledgeable and prepared to follow the ASERVIC Competencies?
6. How are spirituality and multiculturalism connected?
7. How has this activity prepared you to conduct a spiritual assessment?

Adaptations for other course formats:
While this activity can be covered in an asynchronous format, an interactive synchronous or in-person format is preferred.

The Tale of the New Flight Attendant:
An Informed Consent Activity
Elizabeth Brokamp, PhD, LPC, NCC, ACS

Materials needed:
Student handout: The Tale of the New Flight Attendant

Time needed:
45–60 minutes

Learning objectives:
1. Demonstrate knowledge of the ethical and legal components of informed consent by identifying required elements and explaining their importance in counseling.
2. Develop the ability to deliver informed consent information in a way that balances content with engagement, fostering a welcoming and professional atmosphere for clients.
3. Apply the metaphor of the flight attendant safety briefing to identify and practice effective communication strategies, ensuring informed consent delivery is clear, thorough, and client-centered.

Instructions:
1. Introduce students to the concept of informed consent, sharing its function and importance when establishing a relationship with a new client. Explain that informed consent should occur both verbally and through a written disclosure, which is a legal contract. The ACA Code of Ethics (2014) provides a comprehensive list of recommended elements that ethical informed consent should contain:

   • A description of all services provided, the purposes, goals, techniques, procedures, limitations, potential risks, and benefits of services, the counselor's qualifications, credentials, relevant experience, and approach to counseling, continuation of services upon the incapacitation or death of the counselor, the role of technology, the implications of diagnosis and the intended use of tests and reports, fees and billing arrangements, including procedures for nonpayment of fees, the client's right to confidentiality and to be provided with an explanation of its limits (including how supervisors and/or treatment or interdisciplinary team professionals are involved), clear information about their records, the right to participate in the ongoing counseling plans, the right to refuse any services or modality changes and to be advised of the consequences of such refusal, and any other pertinent information (ACA, 2014, A.2.b, p.4).

2. After you have shared the informed consent information, share the metaphorical story: A Tale of a New Flight Attendant and give students time to read and digest it. (Appendix B)

3. Lead a group discussion in which students are asked to consider a list of questions:

   • What attitude does the flight attendant convey about the safety material? Do you get the sense that she sees it as important?
   • How safe would you feel with this flight attendant?
   • Would you feel fully prepared to act on her safety information in an emergency?
   • Would you like to continue on the journey?
   • Would you still feel the same level of excitement about the trip?
   • Would you consider her behavior professional? Ethical? Why or why not?

4. If not elicited in the group discussion, point out parallels between a new flight attendant giving a safety briefing and a new counselor discussing informed consent with a new client.

5. Ask students—either on their own, in dyads, or in small groups—to review the story and think about how they would advise the flight attendant to modify her approach. Students should generate a list of five specific changes they would suggest she make when relaying the safety information that can also be

applied to the process of relaying informed consent information to new clients.

6. Discuss as a class and generate a complete list of the class' ideas for how to deliver safety information in a responsible, professional, and ethical manner.

This lesson can also be extended with a role-play exercise. Decide which elements of ethical informed consent (ACA, 2014, A.2.b, p.4) you would like students to emphasize verbally and share that list with students (a description of the counseling services, fees and billing, and confidentiality and its limits are a good place to start). Ask students to divide into dyads. Partners will work together and take turns playing the roles of counselor and client. The setting is the intake session, and the counselor's task is to communicate the information in the informed consent while also ensuring that they are engaging with the client.

Debrief questions:
1. What kinds of feelings might a client experience about meeting a new counselor for the first time?
2. How might an informed consent process exacerbate or alleviate those feelings?
3. How can a counselor engender feelings of safety in their client through the informed consent process?
4. Break down the term "informed consent" into its two components and consider what each word means individually. What does it mean to be informed? What does it mean to give consent? What new meaning—if any—is added when the two words are combined?
5. Why is it important to have a clear, informative, and thorough informed consent discussion between a counselor and their new client?
6. What qualities do you think differentiate a good informed consent process from a bad one?
7. What do you think about having the counselor read informed consent information from a paper? In what ways could this be problematic? In what ways could it be helpful?

Adaptations for other course formats:

This lesson can be delivered as an announcement, a recorded lecture, or an individual assignment in an asynchronous class; as a group discussion and dyad activity in breakout rooms in a synchronous, virtual class; and as a lecture, discussion, and activity in an in-person class.

Connecting Students to the American Civil Rights Movement (1954–1985)

Chantrelle D. Varnado-Johnson, PhD, LPC-S, BC-TMH, RPT, NCC
Janay Ward, MA, PLPC, NCC

Materials needed:
Access to music player
Access to the Internet
Writing utensils
One piece of multicultural construction paper for each student
Markers
Colored pencils for every student

Time needed:
1.5 hours

Learning objectives:
1. Develop an understanding of the cultural heritage and resilience of clients from African American, African, and Afro-Caribbean backgrounds by engaging with historical and contemporary cultural expressions.
2. Reflect on and identify their own beliefs, biases, and socio-cultural influences regarding racial and social injustices, enhancing self-awareness and empathy toward clients affected by such issues.
3. Practice culturally responsive communication and teamwork skills by collaboratively discussing emotions, experiences, and strategies for supporting clients facing race-based injustices.

Instructions:
1. Watch the instructional clip on how gospel music paralleled the civil rights movement. (15 minutes)
2. Listen to the song "We Shall Overcome" and read the lyrics as the song is playing. (5 minutes)
3. After the song is played, discuss the lyrics and your emotional responses to them. (5 minutes)

4. Draw a picture representing some of the social injustices you see occurring currently in your local communities. Title this experience. (10 minutes)

5. Create a poem about the race-based injustices experienced by clients of African American, African, and Afro-Caribbean descent and how to create positive change. (15 minutes)

6. Break into small groups of 3–4 and share your images and poems with the group. (15 minutes)

7. Process with the students in a large group discussion their thoughts and emotions when working with oppressed clients. (25 minutes)

Debrief questions:

1. How has the experience today connected to current trends in society and in your own lives?

2. What were some of the feelings and emotions that stood out to you as you listened to the song?

3. How are we impacted today by social injustices in our communities?

4. What are some sources of support for when you feel disenfranchised?

5. What did you learn about yourself and your community?

6. In your own words, what would you like to change in our current society to promote racial healing?

7. What is one takeaway from this lesson related to equality?

Adaptations for other course formats:

This activity can be adapted to any course format. For online use, the instructor can use breakout rooms for small emotional discussions, as well as the sharing of images and poems. The instructor can also use Poll Everywhere to show emotions on the screen.

In a synchronous online environment, instructors can instruct the students to come to class prepared with a list of social injustices they see in their lives and community. To deepen discussions, the students would review their lists in breakout rooms.

References

Dr. Ham. (2016, January 18). Civil rights music video "we shall overcome" by Peter Seeger. [Video]. YouTube.https://www.youtube.com/watch?v=4gmTxc2wGTI.

Funky Fly 2. (2010, November 28). From "too close to heaven: The history of gospel music" [Video]. YouTube. https://www.youtube.com/watch?v=jv40KudGG08.

Seeger, P. (1963). We shall overcome. [Lyrics]. https://www.civiced.org/blackmonth/resources/svpdpsitelesson 6/Handout1.pdf

Conducting a Biopsychosocial Assessment

Materials needed:
A case vignette

Time needed:
60 minutes

Learning objectives:
1. Develop the ability to formulate purposeful, open-ended questions that facilitate comprehensive understanding while avoiding unnecessary inquiries.
2. Practice listening attentively to the instructor's role play and think critically about the information provided to guide their questioning effectively.
3. Learn to gather information relevant to the biopsychosocial model, encompassing biological, psychological, and social factors.

Instructions:
1. Introduce the concept of the biopsychosocial model and its importance in counseling. (10 minutes)
2. The instructor will provide an overview of the case, sharing background information as if they are the client. This should include demographic details, presenting concerns, and any relevant history (e.g., medical, psychological, social). (15 minutes)
3. Divide the class into pairs. Each pair is only allowed to ask two questions during their turn. This constraint encourages them to think critically about which questions are most essential. The instructor will answer as if they are the client. (10 minutes)
4. Continue on with the next pair until each pair has asked their two questions. (30 minutes)

Debriefing questions:
1. What were your strategies for selecting your two questions?
2. How did you feel about the limitation of only asking two questions?

3. What types of questions did you find most effective in eliciting useful information?
4. Were there any gaps in the information you gathered? If so, what would you have liked to ask for clarity?
5. How can this exercise inform your future practice in conducting biopsychosocial assessments?

Adaptations for other course formats:

The use of breakout rooms can be utilized for a synchronous online environment. In the asynchronous format, the instructor records a "client role-play" video in which they act as the client and share background information about the case. Students can be assigned to pairs and participate in a discussion board where they are allowed to post two questions. The instructor, still acting as the client, replies with answers.

Embodied Connections: A Role Play to Case Conceptualization

(Hinkle & Dean, 2017)

Materials needed:
Index Cards—Each card should have one psychosocial domain written on it (e.g., presenting problem, trauma history, family, culture, strengths). Fictional Client Case Study—A detailed and identical case study for all groups.
Guiding Questions—A printed or digital handout with reflective and interview prompts for each domain.

Time needed:
90–120 minutes

Learning objectives:
1. Understand the interconnectedness of psychosocial domains in a client's life.
2. Develop empathy for clients by embodying different aspects of their experiences.
3. Practice holistic case conceptualization using an integrated framework.

Instructions:
1. Divide students into groups of 5–6. Each group will work with an identical fictional client case study. (5 minutes)
2. Provide each student with an index card containing one domain of the client's psychosocial history (e.g., presenting problem, trauma history, family, culture, strengths, etc.). (2 minutes)
3. Instruct students to reflect on their assigned domain using guiding questions such as:

    How might the client present this information to a counselor?
    What emotions does this information elicit?
    How might this domain influence other aspects of the client's life?

4. Domain interviews:

    Option 1: Domain Interviews: pair two students, each representing different domains, for a conversation. Observers in the group take notes on the interaction, considering how it contributes to a holistic understanding of the client.

    For example:

    - Trauma and Presenting Problem might discuss questions like:

        ○ What might Trauma be trying to communicate through symptoms?
        ○ What questions might Presenting Problem have for Trauma?

    Option 2: Domain Panels: A student representing one domain (e.g., Culture) interviews a panel of other domains (e.g., Family, Education/Work, and Presenting Problem) with questions like:

    - In what ways does Culture influence you?
    - What challenges or benefits does Culture bring to your interactions?

    Rotate roles so each student participates in both panel and observer roles.

    Option 3: Domain Soliloquy: Each student delivers a 2–3 minute soliloquy in character, sharing insights and perspectives from their domain.

    For example:

    - Strength might say, "I remind her she has overcome challenges before, and I fuel her hope for the future."

    After each soliloquy, group members discuss how the presented domain impacts their own role.

5. Provide students with the full case study. Ask them to relinquish their domain roles and take on the perspective of a counselor. Instruct students to write a holistic conceptualization of the client, incorporating:

- Theory-based conceptualization
- Counselor roles and strategies for effective engagement
- Factors impeding growth
- Factors contributing to growth

Debrief questions:
1. How did embodying a specific domain influence your understanding of the client's experiences?
2. What did you learn about the interconnectedness of different aspects of the client's life?
3. What challenges did you encounter in stepping into your assigned role?
4. How might this activity inform your future practice as a counselor?
5. What insights did you gain about using strengths and resources in case conceptualization?

Adaptations for other course formats:
To adapt this activity for the online environment, use virtual meeting platforms with breakout room capabilities (e.g., Zoom, Microsoft Teams) to facilitate small group interactions. Provide students with digital versions of the client case study domains, distributed via email or through the learning management system (LMS). Utilize breakout rooms for domain-specific role interactions, ensuring each group receives clear instructions and a time limit for discussions. Soliloquies and panels can take place in the main session, with students taking turns presenting while others observe and reflect. Employ shared digital tools, such as Google Docs or Jamboard, for students to collaboratively record their observations and create a comprehensive case conceptualization. Incorporate polling features or chat boxes for real-time responses during the processing phase. To enhance engagement, encourage students to use virtual backgrounds or small props that represent their assigned domains. Finally, ensure sufficient time for debriefing, either synchronously in a group discussion or asynchronously via a reflective discussion board.

Guess and Reflect: Developing Empathy and Feeling Reflection Skills

(Tollenson et al., 2017)

Materials needed:
Notecards (two per participant)
Pens or pencils

Time needed:
60 minutes

Learning objectives:
1. Enhance students' ability to recognize and reflect on emotions through verbal and nonverbal cues.
2. Develop comfort and skill in naming feelings, even when uncertain of accuracy.
3. Build confidence in reflecting client feelings during counseling sessions.

Instructions:
1. Explain the importance of reflecting feelings in counseling practice. Highlight that this activity is designed to provide a nonjudgmental space to practice empathy and reflection skills. (5 minutes)
2. Pair students randomly or allow them to choose a partner. (2 minutes)
3. Provide each dyad with two notecards and pens/pencils. Instruct one student from each dyad to take a couple of minutes to write three feeling words that describe their current emotional state on their notecard (e.g., anxious, content, frustrated). (5 minutes)
4. The student who wrote the feelings selects one feeling to express without directly naming it. Encourage them to use a combination of verbal statements, nonverbal cues (e.g., facial expressions, gestures), and tone of voice. The partner actively listens and attempts to identify the expressed feeling, stating their guess out loud. If the guess is close but not exact, the feeling owner can accept it as a valid approximation. Once all three

feelings are communicated and identified, students switch roles. (15–20 minutes)

5. The process repeats with the other partner as the feeling communicator. (15–20 minutes)

Debriefing questions:

1. In what ways were you able to identify the feelings communicated by your partner?
2. If a mismatch occurred between the feelings you perceived and the one your partner conveyed, what might account for the mismatch?
3. Which cues from your partner did you tend to rely on most or least?
4. What aspects of this activity did you find most easy or most challenging?
5. Where do you see areas for growth in perceiving and reflecting feelings?
6. How does this experience relate to reflecting feelings in actual counseling sessions?

Adaptations to other course formats:

Set up a video conferencing platform with breakout room functionality to facilitate paired interactions. Students will begin by privately writing their feeling words in a personal document or message, which they will then share verbally during the activity. Before sending pairs to breakout rooms, provide clear instructions via screen sharing or the chat feature to ensure participants understand their tasks. Encourage students to emphasize nonverbal communication during their interactions, such as facial expressions and tone of voice, to enhance connection and understanding in the virtual environment. After the activity, facilitate a shared reflection using a collaborative online document or discussion board, allowing participants to debrief and discuss their experiences, especially if synchronous discussion is not possible.

Reference

Tolleson, A. M., Grad, R., Zabek, F., & Zeligman, M. (2017). Teaching helping skills courses: Creative activities to reduce anxiety. *Journal of Creativity in Mental Health*, *12*(4), 428–439.

Nonverbal Communication Puzzle Challenge

Materials needed:
Small puzzles with 25–50 pieces. You can either use physical puzzle pieces or digital puzzles if using computers.

Time needed:
50 minutes

Learning objectives:
1. To help students identify and observe nonverbal counseling skills, such as body language, facial expressions, posture, and eye contact, by working through a puzzle activity that requires interpreting nonverbal cues.
2. This activity provides a hands-on, interactive way for students to observe and discuss nonverbal communication, which is essential for effective counseling. It encourages reflection, active listening, and the practical application of nonverbal skills in real-world settings.

Instructions:
1. Divide the students into small groups (3–5 students per group). (5 minutes)
2. Give each group a puzzle set (either a physical puzzle or a digital version with various images). (5 minutes)
3. Students will work together to complete the puzzle. The twist is that they must not talk while putting the puzzle together. The students need to pay close attention to the nonverbal behaviors of others in their group. (15 minutes)
4. After completing the puzzle, each group will identify and discuss what nonverbal cues they observed in their group members. (10 minutes)
5. Process and share out in a large group. (10 minutes)
6. Summarize the importance of nonverbal communication in counseling, emphasizing that it can often speak louder than words. Encourage students to remain aware of their own nonverbal behaviors and to be observant of clients' cues, as this can significantly enhance the therapeutic process. (5 minutes)

Debriefing questions:
1. What nonverbal cues did you notice?
2. Discuss the specific nonverbal behaviors you observed in the group members (e.g., crossed arms, leaning in, maintaining eye contact).
3. How do you think these nonverbal cues might influence the therapeutic relationship or communication between the counselor and client?
4. How do nonverbal cues affect the counseling session?
5. How did the nonverbal cues of group members suggest emotions, attitudes, or feelings?
6. What role do these nonverbal signals play in conveying empathy, understanding, or concern during counseling?
7. How can nonverbal cues impact trust building in counseling?
8. Did the body language and facial expressions in group members convey warmth and trust, or did they seem distant or closed off? How might this affect a client's willingness to share?
9. Did you observe any discrepancies between verbal and nonverbal communication?
10. While processing in your small groups, were there any moments when the body language or facial expression of group members did not match the verbal message they meant to convey?
11. How might such discrepancies impact the counseling process?
12. What are some nonverbal cues that are often misinterpreted in counseling?
13. Which nonverbal cues are easily misunderstood, and how might they lead to miscommunication or misunderstanding during therapy sessions?
14. How can you, as a counselor, avoid these misinterpretations or manage them if they occur?
15. How can you use nonverbal communication effectively in your own counseling practice?
16. Based on what you observed in the puzzle activity, what nonverbal behaviors would you like to incorporate into your own practice to build rapport and understanding with clients?

17. What are some nonverbal behaviors that you should be aware of and possibly adjust to avoid negative impacts on communication?
18. How can you assess a client's nonverbal cues during a session?
19. What strategies can you use to better observe and respond to nonverbal cues in a counseling session?
20. How can you assess whether your own nonverbal behavior aligns with the messages you are trying to convey to clients?

Adaptations for other course formats:
This activity can be adapted to an online synchronous course format. For online use, the instructor can use breakout rooms to create smaller groups with digital puzzles.

Using I-Poetry for Case Conceptualization and Treatment Planning

(McFarlin & Sartor, 2023)

Materials needed:
A recorded counseling session (with client consent)
Transcription software or a word processor
Printed or digital copies of the Temporal/Contextual (T/C) Model for Case Conceptualization (Zubernis et al., 2017)
Highlighters or annotation tools
Reflective question worksheet

Time needed:
30–60 minutes (reviewing a recorded session and transcribing)
90 minutes (creating the I-Poem, conceptualizing, and reflecting)

Learning objectives:
1. Identify and extract "I" statements from a client's spoken words to enhance understanding of the client's narrative.
2. Apply the **Temporal/Contextual (T/C) Model for Case Conceptualization** to analyze client concerns.
3. Develop treatment plans grounded in a deeper awareness of a client's self-perceptions, emotions, and behaviors.
4. Reflect on personal biases, new insights, and the impact of listening deeply to a client's voice.

Instructions:
1. Preparing the I-Poem Transcript: Have the students listen to the recorded counseling session multiple times to familiarize themselves with the client's narrative. Have them transcribe the entire session, documenting only the client's spoken words in their original order. Have students read through the full transcript, highlighting every first-person statement (I, I'm, I've, I feel, etc.). They will then remove all non-"I" statements, leaving only the client's self-referential statements in sequence.

2. Next, have students group the remaining "I" statements into stanzas based on shifts in meaning, emotion, or themes. They will re-read the I-Poem multiple times and refine the structure to enhance clarity.

3. Use the Temporal/Contextual (T/C) Model for Case Conceptualization to categorize the client's "I" statements into:
    Internal constructs (self-efficacy, self-esteem, beliefs)
    Emotional and behavioral patterns
    Coping mechanisms and strengths
    Cultural and environmental influences
    Timeline influences (past, present, future)

4. Answer the following reflective questions in writing:
    What core themes emerge from the client's I-Poem?
    How does this exercise change your understanding of the client's presenting concerns?
    What treatment focus areas emerge from the I-Poem?
    Which theoretical approach best aligns with this case? Why?
    What interventions are appropriate given the client's needs and readiness for change?
    How has this exercise impacted your empathy or understanding of the client's experience?

5. Develop three targeted interventions based on the conceptualization.

Debriefing questions:

1. How did extracting only the client's "I" statements impact your perception of their experience?

2. What insights about the client's self-concept and emotional state emerged from the I-Poem?

3. How did this activity deepen your understanding of the case conceptualization process?

4. Were there any unexpected revelations that emerged through this exercise?

5. How could using I-Poetry enhance counselor empathy and active listening skills?

Adaptations for online courses:

To adapt this activity for online courses, instructors can provide students with pre-recorded counseling sessions or AI-generated transcripts for analysis, allowing them to engage with case material in a virtual format. Using collaborative Google Docs, students can annotate, edit, and structure their I-Poems together, fostering peer interaction and shared learning. Discussion boards can be utilized to encourage reflection, where students post their I-Poems and provide constructive feedback to their peers. Additionally, synchronous Zoom sessions can be used for live engagement, enabling students to read their I-Poems aloud and discuss their case conceptualization insights in breakout groups, promoting deeper understanding and dialogue.

References

McFarlin, S. L., & Sartor, T. A. (2023). I-poetry as an instructional tool in counselor education. *Journal of Creativity in Mental Health, 18*(2), 288–300. https://doi.org/10.1080/15401383.2021.1950592

Zubernis, L., Snyder, M., & Neale-McFall, C. (2017). Case conceptualization: Improving understanding and treatment with the temporal/contextual model. *Journal of Mental Health Counseling, 39*(3), 181–194. https://doi.org/10.17744/mehc.39.3.01

5

INTEGRATING CREATIVITY INTO COURSE CONTENT

This chapter examines the integration of creative activities into counseling content courses. Incorporating creative activities is particularly important in counseling education, as it embodies the dynamic and client-centered nature of therapeutic work. Creative methods can transform abstract theories into concrete applications, foster discussions on sensitive topics, and provide opportunities for experiential learning. This chapter presents practical activities for integrating creative activities across various content areas, including ethics, multicultural counseling, group dynamics, and assessment. Additionally, it features examples of activities that correspond with specific course objectives, demonstrating how creativity can be tailored to meet academic and professional standards.

As emphasized in the introductory chapters, all activities, themes, and rituals must be grounded in a clear rationale and aligned with course standards. Chapter 1 guides the intentional design and implementation of creative activities to ensure that they effectively contribute to learning outcomes. Moreover, Chapter 1 emphasizes the importance of creating a

 DOI: 10.4324/9781003514718-5

safe and supportive learning environment where students feel comfortable taking risks and exploring new ideas. It discusses ways to scaffold creative activities to accommodate varying levels of comfort and skill, ensuring that all students benefit from the experience.

Analysis of a Snickers Bar

Suzanne M. Dugger, EdD, NCC, ACS, LPC

Materials needed:
Optional: space to brainstorm ideas, digital ways to provide visual examples.

As a fun optional material, the instructor may bring fun-size Snickers bars to class to share (assuming no peanut allergies).

Time needed:
30 minutes

Learning objectives:
1. Identify and categorize occupations within the six RIASEC types, demonstrating their understanding of Holland's typology and how it relates to real-world work environments.
2. Work collaboratively in small groups to brainstorm and identify diverse occupations, fostering teamwork and innovative problem-solving skills.
3. Explore the variety of roles involved in producing, marketing, and distributing a product, understanding how different occupations contribute to a shared goal within an industry.

Instructions:
1. Prior to introducing this activity, the instructor will teach students about Holland's typology of people and model work environments. This introduction should include Holland's hexagon and the RIASEC types.
2. Have students create groups. Dyads, triads, or small groups will work best.
3. Inform students that they will have 10 minutes to identify at least three (3) occupations in each of the six RIASEC types that would be involved in the production, marketing, and distribution of a Snickers Bar.

4. Optional: Distribute a worksheet on which students can record their brainstormed ideas.

5. After 10 minutes, reconvene the class.

6. Focusing on one RIASEC type at a time, invite students to share the occupations they brainstormed. If desired, after students have shared their ideas, share an animated PPT slide with visual examples of numerous occupations that would be involved in the production, marketing, and distribution of a Snickers Bar, again focusing on one RIASEC type at a time. Some ideas are included below:

   • Realistic—Student ideas followed by instructor examples on a PPT

     ◦ Farm Workers (image of peanut farmers)
     ◦ Production Workers (image of production workers)
     ◦ Truck Drivers (image of Snickers truck)
     ◦ Custodial Workers (image of clean Snickers production facility)

   • Investigative–Student ideas followed by instructor examples on a PPT

     ◦ Chocolate Taster
     ◦ Food Safety Scientist (image of MARS website page about food safety)
     ◦ Market Research Analysts
     ◦ Quality Control Analysts
     ◦ Mechanical Engineers
     ◦ Packaging Technology Engineer
     ◦ Sustainability—Wind Farm Engineers (image of website about MARS' goal of becoming carbon neutral by 2040)

   • Artistic–Student ideas followed by instructor examples on a PPT

     ◦ Actors (image or video of a Snickers commercial)
     ◦ Creative Directors

- ○ Fashion Designers
- ○ Film and Video Editors
- ○ Graphic Designers

- Social—Student ideas followed by instructor examples on a PPT

  - ○ Consumer Psychologist
  - ○ Customer Service Representatives
  - ○ Training and Development Specialists

- Enterprising—Student ideas followed by instructor examples on a PPT

  - ○ Advertising and Promotions Manager
  - ○ Chief Executives
  - ○ Marketing Managers
  - ○ Public Relations Specialists
  - ○ Search Marketing Strategists

- Conventional—Student ideas followed by instructor examples on a PPT

  - ○ Accountants
  - ○ Production, Planning, and Expediting Clerks
  - ○ Secretaries and Administrative Assistants
  - ○ Shipping Clerk
  - ○ Web Administrators and Developers

Debrief questions:
1. How has this activity helped you to master the meaning of the RIASEC types?
2. What are your major takeaways from this activity?
3. How could you use a similar activity to emphasize the wide variety of careers associated with a specific organization (e.g., Apple or Google) or a specific industry (e.g., professional sports)?

Adaptations for other course formats:

In preparation for doing this activity with a synchronous online course, extend an invitation in the previous class session for students to bring a Snickers bar to class (without telling them why). You can utilize a break-out room in a synchronous online course for the brainstorming sessions and disseminate the worksheet via that.

Drawing: The Ideal vs. Real Counseling Graduate Student

Xiaoxuan Qu, PhD; and Melissa Luke, PhD, LMHC, NCC, ACS

Materials needed:
Blackboard/whiteboard
Chalk/markers

Time needed:
30 minutes

Learning objectives:
1. Explore and articulate the differences between their perceptions of an ideal graduate student and the reality of their own experiences, promoting self-awareness and reflection.
2. Collaborate in small groups to express their ideas creatively through drawing and discussion, enhancing their ability to work together and communicate their thoughts effectively.

Instructions:
1. Divide the group into two. If the number of students exceeds 10, multiple groups can be considered. (1–2 minutes)
2. Ask one group to draw an image of an ideal graduate student and ask the other group to draw an image of a real graduate student. (5 minutes)
3. After the drawing is finished, ask group members to compare and contrast the two images. (2 minutes)
4. Give group members opportunities to elaborate on their musings within the group. (10 minutes)
5. Come back to the whole class and show processing questions (see below). (1 minute)
6. Ask students to choose one or two questions to answer. (10 minutes)

Debrief questions:
1. What was your experience doing this activity?
2. What thoughts and emotions came to you in the process?

3. Comparing the two pictures, what are some of your reactions?
4. What did you learn about yourself in this process?
5. What did you learn about your peers in this process?
6. What are you deciding about yourself as a graduate student in the upcoming months?

Adaptations for other course formats:

This drawing activity can be adapted to a virtual format in which students are grouped into breakout rooms and utilize online platforms, such as FigJam, to make drawings. In addition, this activity can be assigned as an asynchronous assignment in which students are asked to complete the two images on their own and make comparisons.

Creating Personality: An Adlerian Perspective

Xiaoxuan Qu, PhD; and Melissa Luke, PhD, LMHC, NCC, ACS

Materials needed:
The "Creative force": How Children Create Their Personalities (Bettner, 2006)

Time needed:
30—50 minutes

Learning objectives:
1. Analyze personality development through the lens of Adlerian by engaging with the *Creative Force* to enhance their understanding of theoretical constructs and their application to real-life scenarios.
2. Bridge theoretical knowledge and practical application by reflecting on Adlerian concepts and applying them to case conceptualization and client understanding.
3. Improve their ability to articulate theoretical ideas in writing and discussion through reflective responses to processing questions, fostering critical thinking and professional language development.

Instructions:
1. Assign reading the *Creative Force: How Children Create Their Personalities* as an assignment. Alternatively, read the book together in class. (10–15 minutes)
2. As part of the assignment, instruct students to write a reflection paper by responding to the processing questions (see below). Alternatively, ask students to pick one processing question to respond. (20–35 minutes)

Debrief questions:
1. Which Adlerian constructs can you identify from this book?
2. Through the case illustration of a girl named Susie in this book, in what ways has your theoretical understanding of personality development deepened?

3. Which elements in the book stand out to you the most?
4. Which parts remain confusing or intriguing?
5. To what extent is Adlerian Psychology inclusive or exclusive to diverse client populations?
6. What is important to you when it comes to choosing your preferred counseling theoretical orientation(s)?

Special considerations:
This book should be read with caution, as its gender identity only includes male and female. Counselor educators can turn this feature into a learning opportunity. One example is introducing Erik Mansager's (2008) article on affirming lesbian, gay, bisexual, and transgender individuals.

Adaptations for other course formats:
Counselor educators can incorporate this book into a learning activity in the classroom, where students actively participate in reading together. This activity can be easily adapted into a course announcement or discussion board.

References

Bettner, B. L. (2006). *The "creative force": How children create their personalities.* Author.

Mansager, E. (2008). Affirming lesbian, gay, bisexual, and transgender individuals. *The Journal of Individual Psychology, 64*(2), 123–136.

Personal Guiding Theory Visual Representation

Amy Barth, PhD, LPC (WI), LCPC (IL)

Materials needed:
No materials are specifically specified. Because students do the work on their own, they choose what, if any materials they would like to use. If you were to do this activity during a class, you will want to either have some arts and crafts materials on hand or have students use virtual resources.

Time needed:
Have students do it on their own time
2 hours (in class)

Learning objectives:
1. Synthesize their values, beliefs, and understanding of theoretical frameworks.
2. To begin developing a personal guiding theory of counseling that aligns with their professional identity.
3. Demonstrate their ability to articulate how people grow, develop, and change by creating a visual representation that reflects their personal philosophy and its alignment with counseling theories.
4. Engage with the counseling relationship's role in facilitating change through reflective exploration and visual representation of their emerging personal guiding theory.

Instructions:
1. Students will express their current understanding of their personal guiding theory of counseling through a visual representation. This can be achieved by creating or incorporating various forms of media such as drawing, painting, collage, Prezi, video, photographs, or physical objects. Students are encouraged to either create something original, utilize an existing item that resonates with their theory, or combine both approaches to develop a meaningful and personalized representation. The goal

is to creatively convey their guiding theory to reflect their unique perspective and evolving identity as a counselor.

2. Students then either bring their visual or a picture of the visual to class. In a round-robin style, students informally share their visuals and descriptions.

Debrief questions:

1. Describe the developmental process that happened for you this semester in developing your current identification of a personal guiding theory of counseling?

2. What has been most significant for you in this developmental process?

3. What did you learn about yourself as a person and as a professional counselor throughout this developmental process?

4. How does your current identification of a personal guiding theory of counseling align with how you see yourself as a person and as a counselor?

5. How do you see your personal guiding theory continuing to evolve in the future?

Rational Emotive Behavioral Therapy (REBT) Role Playing with "Thought-Exchange"

Dhionis Tartari, LPC, BC-TMH

Materials needed:
Index cards
Pens
Role-playing scenarios based on common irrational beliefs
Whiteboard or flip chart
Markers

Time needed:
1.5 hours

Learning objectives:
1. Demonstrate understanding of the ABCDE model of REBT by identifying and disputing irrational beliefs through role playing and interactive scenarios.
2. Develop practical counseling skills by applying REBT techniques in small-group role plays, enhancing their ability to support clients in reframing irrational beliefs and achieving emotional and behavioral change.
3. Engage in collaborative learning and critical thinking by analyzing diverse approaches to disputing irrational beliefs, providing constructive feedback, and reflecting on the effectiveness of applied techniques in a group setting.

Instructions:
1. Begin by explaining the fundamentals of REBT, particularly the ABCDE model (Ellis and Dryden, 2007), emphasizing the importance of identifying and disputing irrational beliefs to help clients achieve emotional and behavioral change. (10 minutes)

    ABCDE Model (Short Form):

    • A—Activating Event: An event that triggers an emotional response.

- B—Beliefs: The irrational beliefs about the activating event.
- C—Consequences: The emotional and behavioral consequences of the irrational beliefs.
- D—Disputation: Challenging the irrational beliefs to change them.
- E—Effect: The new, healthier emotional and behavioral outcome after disputing the beliefs.

Common Disputation Questions to Challenge Irrational Beliefs

- Is this belief based on objective reality or personal opinion?
- What evidence do you have that this belief is true?
- How is this belief helping or hindering you in achieving your goals?
- Why must things be the way you believe they should be?
- Are you demanding certainty or perfection in an uncertain and imperfect world?
- How does this belief influence your emotions and behaviors?

2. Divide the class into small groups (4–6), pairs (dyads), or triads, depending on the class size, to facilitate more intimate and focused interactions. (5 minutes)
3. Provide each group with a set of role-playing scenarios written on index cards, each depicting common irrational beliefs. Explain that each group will role-play these scenarios to practice REBT techniques. (5 minutes)

Common Irrational Beliefs for Scenarios:

- "I must be liked by everyone to feel good about myself."
- "If I make a mistake, it means I am a failure."
- "People should treat me fairly at all times."
- "I can't stand it when things don't go my way."
- "I should be perfect in everything I do."
- "It's terrible when things are not the way I want them to be."
- "I must have immediate solutions to my problems."
- "I am worthless if I am not successful in all areas of life."
- "I cannot be happy unless I am in control of every situation."
- "I must always win others' approval."

4. Instruct groups to assign roles within each group: a client, a counselor, and one or more observers. The "client" reads the scenario aloud, expressing the irrational belief, while the "counselor" uses REBT techniques to dispute the belief. Observers take notes on the interaction, focusing on the use of REBT skills and providing feedback afterward. (20 minutes)

5. After the initial role plays, each group writes down the irrational belief discussed on an index card. Groups then exchange cards with another group, requiring the new "counselor" to address the irrational belief received from the other group. This promotes flexibility and adaptability in applying REBT techniques. (20 minutes)

6. Reconvene as a large group and have each group share their experiences, focusing on the challenges faced and the strategies used. Facilitate a discussion on the different approaches and solutions observed during the role plays. (15 minutes)

Debrief questions:
1. What irrational beliefs did you encounter during the role plays?
2. How did you identify the irrational beliefs in the scenarios?
3. Which disputing techniques were most effective, and why?
4. How did the "Thought-Exchange" technique enhance your understanding of REBT principles?
5. What challenges did you face in disputing irrational beliefs, and how did you overcome them?
6. How can you apply the REBT techniques practiced today in real counseling sessions?
7. How did this activity enhance your understanding of REBT and its application?
8. What did you learn about your own professional dispositions during this exercise?
9. How can you incorporate these REBT skills into your future counseling practice?
10. What feedback did you receive from your peers, and how will it influence your approach moving forward?

Adaptations for other course formats:

In an asynchronous environment, provide pre-recorded scenarios and detailed instructions. Students can record their role-playing sessions and submit them for instructor feedback. Use an online discussion board for students to share their experiences and reflections, fostering an interactive learning environment even in an asynchronous format. For the virtual platform, utilize breakout rooms for small group role-playing sessions. Digital tools, such as Google Docs, can be used to share and exchange scenarios among groups. Facilitate the debriefing session through a virtual meeting platform, ensuring all students can participate in the discussion.

Reference

Ellis, A., & Dryden, W. (2007). *The practice of rational emotive behavior therapy.* Springer Publishing Company.

A Sensory-Based Wellness Experience in Counselor Training

Elizabeth A. Keller-Dupree, PhD, LPC-S, NCC

Materials needed:
One blank 8 × 11 sheet of paper per student *or* a copy of the Sensual Awareness Inventory (Burns, 1998)

Time needed:
1 hour

Learning objectives:
1. Identify and analyze sensory experiences that contribute to positive emotions, enhancing their understanding of how sensory inputs influence emotional well-being and support the Broaden-and-Build Theory of Positive Emotion.
2. Students will reflect on and articulate the relationship between sensory awareness and personal wellness, fostering deeper self-awareness of the activities and experiences that enhance their emotional and physical well-being.
3. Students will develop professional competency in facilitating experiential sensory interventions, equipping them to apply the SAI or similar techniques within their future counseling practices to promote client well-being across diverse populations.

Instructions:
1. Instruct students that one way to consider how we individually achieve positive emotions is to first deconstruct our daily experiences into our five senses of sight, sound, touch, taste, and smell, with special attention to moments when we feel an "affective lift." For some individuals, that "affective lift" will feel peaceful or comforting, while for others, that lift may feel happy or joyful. The introduction to this activity can be used as an instructional document for this step. (5 minutes)

2. Distribute the sensual awareness inventory (Burns, 1998). For those who are not able to access the inventory, distribute a white piece of 8½ × 11 paper to each student. Students can fold the paper lengthwise, followed by folding it into thirds, making six equal rectangles when the paper is unfolded. Students can then be instructed to write the words "sight," "sound," "touch," "taste," "smell," and "activity," with one word being assigned to each box. (5 minutes)

3. Explain the following: "Under each heading, please list about 10 items or activities from which you receive pleasure, enjoyment, happiness, joy, comfort, or another positive affective feeling." The faculty member may model how to complete one of the rectangles by stating, "For example, if I am completing the taste rectangle, things I taste that bring me joy are pizza sauce, medium roast coffee, lemon-flavored desserts, coconut, etc." Invite students to thoughtfully consider the deconstruction of each sense for a full experience of the individual senses. (25 minutes)

4. Facilitate a large group discussion using debriefing questions to explore the insights and impacts of the activity. (25 minutes)

Debrief questions:
1. When completing the activity, which positive affective word did you use to fill in the blank in each sensory box?
2. What trends or themes do you notice across your senses?
3. Which sense(s) came most readily (easily) to you?
4. Which sense(s) was/were the most challenging for you to identify?
5. How might these sensory experiences differ if this activity was completed six months from now?
6. In what ways do you nurture these sensory experiences currently?
7. In what ways have these sensory experiences been neglected?
8. If you could implement one change today to increase the positive emotion you experience from a sense, what change would you target?

Adaptations for other course formats:
This activity can be facilitated in-person or online (synchronously or asynchronously). For asynchronous settings, students can reflect on the debriefing questions through a reflection paper (four page minimum) that is then reviewed and responded to by the faculty member. For synchronous instruction (in-person or online), this activity may be debriefed within a whole-class setup, with the faculty member asking the questions to all students simultaneously. Alternatively, for synchronous instruction, students may work in small groups (up to five people), with each group member taking a turn facilitating a debriefing question.

Reference

Burns, G. (1998). *Nature guided therapy: Brief integrative strategies for health and well being* (1st ed.). Taylor & Francis. https://doi.org/10.4324/9781315803586

Final Theories Podcast

Ashton Keys, MS, NCC
Emeline Eckart, PhD

Materials needed:
Access to Zoom and/or podcast recording software

Time needed:
20 minutes

Learning objectives:

1. Demonstrate a comprehensive understanding of their chosen counseling theory, including its core principles and techniques, by articulating its application to treating clients with anxiety disorders during a collaborative podcast recording.
2. Compare and contrast two counseling theories, exploring their respective strengths and limitations in addressing client needs while fostering dialogue and collaboration with peers.
3. Professional communication skills by presenting theoretical concepts in an accessible and engaging format, enhancing their ability to explain and advocate for their chosen theory in real-world counseling scenarios.

Instructions:

1. Students will select one theory explored in the course that they will likely incorporate into their future practice.
2. Students will be paired with another student who has a different selected theory.
3. The pairs will take on the persona of a counselor proficient in their chosen theory and record a 10–15-minute podcast discussing and comparing theoretical techniques with their partner on how their theory can be used to work with a client diagnosed with an anxiety disorder.
4. Partners will create an engaging title for their podcast episode and upload their recording to a classroom forum.

Debrief questions:
1. Describe the key concepts of your chosen theory.
2. What populations does your theory best serve?
3. Describe the interventions most commonly associated with your chosen theory.
4. Compare and contrast your chosen theory with your partner's theory.
5. Describe the benefits and challenges of both your and your partner's theory.
6. Identify at least three takeaways from the podcast activity that you can use in your future counseling practice.

Adaptations for other course formats:
This activity is appropriate for face-to-face, virtual, or asynchronous classroom formats.

A Tripartite Creative Fieldwork Activity

Using Qualitative Analysis to Facilitate
Counselors-in-Training Self-Efficacy

Cortny Stark (she/her), PhD, LPCC, LADAC, CRC
Emma Vdoviak-Markow (she/her), MA, LPCC-S, LMFT-S, NCC,
ACS, PhD, Counselor Education Student

Materials needed:
Assignment Instructions for Self-Efficacy Reflection Paper—one per student
Self-Efficacy Scale (Lent et al., 2003)—one per student
Memo—Summary of Coding Impressions—one per student.

Student provided materials:
Self-Efficacy Reflection Paper (digital or hardcopy provided to instructor)

Time needed:
Approximately 1.5 hours at the beginning of the semester to complete the review of coding themes in class. Several weeks later, 1 hour of class time will be needed to review the codes and engage in class discussion of assignment experiences and codes.

Between these two classes, students will need additional time to complete and submit their Self-Efficacy Scale (Lent et al., 2003) and self-reflection paper, and the instructor will need time outside of class to grade and code the reflection papers and summarize the findings into a PowerPoint or other presentation format.

Learning objectives:
1. Demonstrate increased self-awareness and confidence in their abilities as counselors-in-training.
2. Critically reflect on their experiences and responses, using instructor feedback and peer interaction to identify and process primary themes related to their development as clinicians.
3. Enhance their understanding of imposter syndrome and personal challenges in counseling practice through class discussion

and analysis of their own and their peers' experiences, promoting growth in self-efficacy and self-awareness.

Instructions:

1. This activity is facilitated during students' internship experience and consists of three core components conducted at different times throughout the semester. The first component is the assignment, which is provided to students in the syllabus and discussed during the initial class session. Once students have submitted their completed assignments, the instructor reviews them for grading purposes and briefly codes student responses to identify themes. The final portion of the activity involves processing the identified themes (without disclosing which students discussed which themes) as a large group during scheduled class time.

2. Students are provided with a copy of the assignment instructions on the first day of class and are given approximately four weeks to complete it. The assignment requires completing the Self-Efficacy Scale (Lent et al., 2003) and a one to three-paragraph reflection paper. While completing the paper, students discuss new information they learned about themselves while completing and reviewing their responses to the Self-Efficacy Scale (Lent et al., 2003). They also describe anticipated areas of growth and any efforts they plan to engage in to invest in this growth. Assignment instructions are listed below:

   - Complete the Self-Efficacy Scale (Lent et al., 2003).
   - Download and/or print the form and complete the scale assessment.
   - Write a reflection on the experience and what you learned.

     ○ This reflection should:

       ▪ Be about 1–3 paragraphs
       ▪ Discuss new information you learned about yourself (e.g. "I hadn't realized that I didn't feel comfortable with ____ and _____ counseling skills!")

- Discuss anticipated areas of growth and/or interventions to promote growth (e.g. "now that I know that I don't feel very confident with these skills, I plan to look up texts—like ____[insert book title here]____—and do some more research on the topic. I also plan to talk with my site supervisor about how I might practice these skills at my site, or possible professional development opportunities")

3. Once all students have submitted the completed Self-Efficacy Scale (Lent et al., 2003) and their reflection papers, the instructor reviews the submissions to assign grades and briefly code the student reflections. Part Two usually occurs during the fifth week of the semester. The coding process draws from Dillon's (2012) grounded theory approach to qualitative data analysis by initially engaging in open coding to identify key concepts, followed by axial coding to explore relationships between these concepts, and concluding with selective coding that identifies core groupings or "concepts" emerging from the reflection papers. While reviewing the reflection papers and performing this coding process, the instructor keeps a log of notes or a "memo," documenting the most prominent concepts and relationships.

4. Following completion of the memo, the instructor uses the concepts and relationships between themes to guide preparations for class. The instructor utilizes the themes and concepts identified while coding students' assignments to create a matrix of feedback that articulates responses to the following questions (adapted from Brooks and colleagues [2019]):

- Feeding up—Where am I going? Describe where we anticipate counselors-in-training to be by the time they complete this semester of fieldwork, specifically regarding their knowledge, skills, awareness, and self-efficacy in the areas articulated in the Self-Efficacy Scales (Lent et al., 2003).
- Feeding back—How am I going? The instructor shares the key concepts and relationships identified during the coding process and how these relate to counselor-in-training

development. For example, the instructor might discuss session mapping (Partridge, 2007) and how this evolves with practice, or imposter syndrome, and how it is disproportionately experienced by persons with marginalized identities.

- Feeding forward—Where to go next? While completing their self-reflection papers, students are asked to identify their next steps for growing their confidence and self-efficacy regarding specific counseling skills and areas of knowledge. Themes identified by the instructor in students' reflection papers are summarized for the class. An example of this might include students' descriptions of core areas they wish to grow in and efforts they plan to engage in, such as finding literature, training, consultation, and supervision.

Debrief questions:
1. What new information did you learn about yourself, your peers, and the counselor development process?
2. What areas of growth do you plan to focus on during the remainder of your fieldwork experience?
3. How will you invest in this growth?
4. How can your instructor support your growth in these areas?
5. How can your classmates support your growth in these areas?
6. How can your site supervisor support your growth in these areas?
7. What challenges or barriers might inhibit your efforts to address these areas of growth, and how will you address them?

Adaptations for other course formats:
This activity may be completed in asynchronous, virtual, or in-person format and can be completed in large and small groups. No additional adaptations are needed to conduct it virtually or in person.

To adapt this activity for asynchronous learning, the instructor will need to utilize all digital documents/files and may transition the "Memo—Summary of Coding Findings" and the "debrief questions" to a discussion board format using the appropriate learning management system (LMS). This will allow students to review the summary of findings and consider how these themes reflect their and their classmates' experiences.

References

Brooks, C., Carroll, A., Gillies, R. M., & Hattie, J. (2019). A matrix of feedback for learning. *Australian Journal of Teacher Education*, *44*(4), 14–32. https://doi.org/10.14221/ajte.2018v44n4.2

Dillon, D. R. (2012). *Grounded theory and qualitative research*. Blackwell Publishing Ltd.

Lent, R. W., Hill, C. E., & Hoffman, M. A. (2003). Counselor Activity Self-Efficacy Scales (CASES) [Database record]. APA PsycTests. https://doi.org/10.1037/t00084-000

Nguyen, L. T. (2023). *Development and validation of the counseling imposter scale (Publication No. 30567081)* [Doctoral Dissertation, Texas A&M University]. ProQuest Dissertations & Theses Global.

Partridge, K. (2007). Holding onto fragments: reflections on using mind maps in therapy. *Context Magazine*, *93*, 22–26.

Cultural Self Portrait

Dan Summer, PhD, LAC, ATR-BC, LPAT, LCAT, ATCS;
Annette Vaccaro, EdD, LPAT, LPC, ATR-BC, ATCS, ACS;
Traci Bitondo, PhD, LPC, LPAT, ATR-BC, ACS, ATCS

Materials needed:
Any art materials for two- or three-dimensional surfaces (fluid materials, paint, markers, watercolor, resistive crayons, pastels, pencils, additional fabric arts, epoxies, etc.)
Paper or canvas 12 × 18, but can be modified
Digital programs (i.e., Procreate)

Time needed:
1–1.5 hours for a family interview
1.5–2.5 hours self-portrait

Learning objectives:
1. Critically examine their own cultural identities using the ADDRESSING Model as a framework to explore intersections of privilege and marginalization, fostering deeper self-awareness and cultural humility.
2. Create an artistic representation of their cultural identities by integrating insights from their family interviews and personal reflections, demonstrating an ability to synthesize intergenerational and individual narratives into a cohesive self-portrait.
3. Engage in peer dialogue and reflection to compare and contrast cultural self-portraits, promoting empathy, openness, and an enriched understanding of diverse perspectives and identities.

Instructions:
1. Provide an overview of the activity, emphasizing the importance of cultural humility, self-reflection, and understanding privilege and marginalization. Introduce the ADDRESSING Model (Hays, 2016), explaining the dimensions of identity: Age, Disability, Disability Later in Life, Race, Ethnicity, Sexual

Orientation, Socioeconomic Status, Indigenous Background, and Gender.

2. Students will select a family member to interview who can provide a narrative of family lineage and culture. The interview will explore current and intergenerational values, beliefs, and attitudes the family holds. Questions may also explore cultural symbols, rituals, artifacts, artistic practices, religious values, and symbols. This allows the student to explore which aspects of cultural identity are salient or not salient to them. (Approximately 10 questions, one hour to one and a half hours in total)

3. Students will create an art piece outside of the classroom using materials of their choice, engaging with their family members' narrative and incorporating elements of their own identity. The project aims to highlight the students' artistic identity as well.

   • It is preferred for students to create a two-dimensional image, but this is not a requirement.
   • The final product does not need to look like a traditional self-portrait but more like an accurate representation of the multiple identities one carries.
   • Students are encouraged to explore using multiple art materials, which may help uncover different feelings, memories, and sensations that can contribute to the creative process and deepen the capacity for self-reflection.
   • Students are encouraged to depict aspects of their identities that are privileged and marginalized.

4. Students will consult with the ADDRESSING model (Hays, 2016) as a guide to include preferred and/or non-preferred aspects of their identity in their art piece.

5. Students will engage in dialogue with peers' cultural self-portraits to capture different perspectives and learn more about their peers' identities.
   (Depending on the accessibility of materials and the desired intentional outcome, the creative process could take between 1.5 and 2.5 hours)

Debrief questions:

1. How did you represent the various dimensions of your cultural identity from the ADDRESSING model in your self-portrait?

2. Which aspects of your identity did you highlight the most in your self-portrait? Why? Which aspects of identity are most salient to you? Least salient? Why? Has this changed throughout your life?

3. Address changes in your worldview that occurred due to your process of identity development.

4. What strategies can you use to continue developing cultural competence in your personal and professional life?

5. Do all aspects of your identity support the same worldview?

6. How did your experiences of power, privilege, and oppression influence your self-portrait?

7. What cultural components are visible? Which are invisible? Does it make a difference?

8. How did you represent chosen, inherited, and imposed components of your culture in your self-portrait?

9. What feelings did you experience while creating your self-portrait, and how did you express them in your artwork?

10. Do we adopt the cultural identities of others? (Family, extended family, friends, teachers, coworkers?) Is this visible in your portrait?

Reference

Hays, P. A. (2016). *Addressing cultural complexities in practice: Assessment, diagnosis, and therapy* (3rd ed.). American Psychological Association. https://doi.org/10.1037/14801-000

Exploring My Racial, Ethnic, and Cultural Identity

Philippa Chin, PhD, LPC, LMFT, NCC
Yahyahan Aras, PhD

Materials needed:
The Exploring My Racial, Ethnic, and Cultural Identity Table
Pen or pencil

Time needed:
1 hour to 1.5 hours per phase

Learning objectives:

1. Reflect on and articulate the visible, partially visible, and hidden aspects of personal racial, ethnic, and cultural identities using the Sunlight, Twilight, and Midnight Zones framework.
2. Analyze how personal heritage, cultural identities, and social experiences influence individual worldviews and interactions with clients from diverse backgrounds.
3. Identify opportunities to apply insights from self-reflection to promote cultural humility, social justice, and anti-racism within counseling practice.

Instructions:

Phase 1: Using Table 5.1 students will list or define their racial, ethnic, and cultural identities. It is okay if students are unable to complete each section. Phase 1 can be completed as one exercise or divided into three exercises over three classes.

1. Starting with the Sunlight zone, students are asked to define their race, ethnicity, and culture as seen by most of the public or most people (receives the most sunlight). (5–10 minutes)
2. For the Twilight Zone, students are asked to define their race, ethnicity, and culture as viewed by a few people (receives little sunlight). (5–10 minutes)
3. Finally, for the Midnight Zone, students are asked to define the areas of their race, ethnicity, and culture that are not seen by others (receive no sunlight/darkness). (5–10 minutes)

4. Sharing and discussion utilizing the debrief questions. (15–30 minutes)

Table 5.1 Phase 1: Exploring My Racial, Ethnic, and Cultural Identity

	Race	Ethnicity	Culture
Sunlight Zone			
Twilight Zone			
Midnight Zone			

Phase 2: beliefs, bias, and prejudice

Using Table 5.2, each student will list or define their beliefs, biases (preferences), and prejudices (opinions without facts) as they relate to their own race, ethnicity, and culture. Beliefs correspond to the sunlight zone, while biases correspond to the twilight zone, and prejudices correspond to the aphotic zone. It is acceptable if students cannot complete each section. Phase 2 can be carried out as a single exercise or divided into three exercises over three classes.

1. Starting with the Sunlight or Beliefs zone, students are asked to write down/list how their personal beliefs about their own race, ethnicity, and culture are seen by or shared with a majority of the public or most people (receives the most sunlight). (5–10 minutes)
2. For the Twilight or Biases zone, students are asked to write down/list their personal biases about their own race, ethnicity, and culture as seen by or shared with a few people (receives little sunlight). (5–10 minutes)
3. Finally for the Midnight or Prejudice zone, students are asked to write down/list their personal prejudices about their own race, ethnicity, and culture that are not seen by others (receives no sunlight/darkness). (5–10 minutes)
4. Sharing and discussion utilizing the debrief questions to follow. * This part does not need to be shared by those who do not wish to. (15–30 minutes)

Table 5.2 Phase 2: Exploring My Racial, Ethnic, and Cultural Identity

	Race	Ethnicity	Culture
Beliefs/Sunlight Zone			
Bias/Twilight Zone			
Prejudice/Midnight Zone			

Phase 3: social justice, advocacy, and anti-racism

Using Table 5.3, each student will explore social justice, advocacy, and anti-racism topics as they relate to race, ethnicity, and culture. Social justice correlates with the sunlight zone. Advocacy correlates with the twilight zone, and anti-racism correlates with the midnight zone. It is okay if students are unable to complete each section. Phase 3 can be completed as one exercise or divided into three exercises over three classes.

1. Starting with the Sunlight or Social Justice zone, students are asked to write down/list current social justice issues related to race, ethnicity, and culture in their community. What is seen and experienced by the public (receives the most sunlight)? Examples could include racial discrimination, lack of access to mental health services for marginalized groups, or cultural insensitivity in therapy practices. (5–10 minutes)
2. For the Twilight or Advocacy zone, students are asked to write down/list ways and strategies of addressing social justice issues. What actions are taken by some people to make social change (receives little sunlight)? (5–10 minutes)
3. Finally for the Midnight or Anti-Racism zone, students are asked to write down or list how the identified social justice issues and strategies of addressing these social justice issues may be rooted in anti-racism. Students are therefore asked to further develop their social justice advocacy awareness by identifying and developing strategies for dismantling oppression rooted in racism. (5–10 minutes)
4. Sharing and discussion utilizing the debrief questions to follow. (15–30 minutes)

Table 5.3 Phase 3: Exploring My Racial, Ethnic, and Cultural Identity

	Race	Ethnicity	Culture
Social/Sunlight Zone			
Advocacy/Twilight Zone			
Anti-Racism/Midnight Zone			

Debrief questions:
1. What came up for you during this activity?
2. What are some of the racial or cultural aspects that you experience in your daily life?
3. How were you socialized around your racial, ethnic, or cultural identities?
4. How does your own racial/ethnic/cultural identity development enter the classroom/your graduate learning experience?
5. How do you think your own racial/ethnic/cultural identity development will impact the counseling space?
6. How do your own beliefs, biases or prejudices enter the classroom/your graduate learning experience?
7. How might your beliefs, biases, or prejudices impact the counseling space?
8. What is your understanding of the differences in social justice, advisory, and anti-racism as they relate to race, ethnicity, and culture?
9. How will you use any new awareness or self-reflection in addressing oppression?
10. How would you describe any changes to your understanding of race, ethnicity, and culture over the course of the activity?

Faculty development and teaching considerations:
The instructor should have a higher ethnic and racial identity development level and applicability experience in comparison to the students. The instructor should be mindful of the differences in ethnic and racial identity development levels of the students and be intentional in demonstrating patience and clarity with instructions. The instructor should be

mindful of power dynamics and cultural differences that might serve as barriers to implementing this activity. The instructor may need to lead by example in sharing about their own identity.

Adaptations for other course formats:
For asynchronous and virtual courses, debrief questions may be presented and commented on through the discussion boards of a learning management system. Instructors may use teaching supports such as Word Cloud to encourage sharing in virtual or in-person classes to support students who are less likely to engage in verbal discussion.

Impromptu Tools for Relationship Building
Sarah Lendt, EdD, LSC, LPCC, NCC

Materials needed:
A randomly chosen item from home

Time needed:
2.5–3 hours

Learning objectives:
1. Demonstrate the ability to creatively use objects or activities to build rapport and connection with children and adolescents by designing and presenting relationship-building tools suited to specific age groups and client needs.
2. Apply developmental theories to assess the appropriateness of different activities for various age groups.
3. Reflect on the importance of flexibility and creativity in the counseling relationship, discussing how relationship-building activities contribute to the therapeutic alliance.

Instructions:
1. Ask students to bring an object from home. The object can be anything they are willing to carry.
2. Once class has begun, students will be asked to consider how the object can be used as a game or activity to build rapport with a student. They will be given a short time to plan, and then they will present their object to the class.
3. Students will be given a short time to plan the presentation of their item. (15 minutes)
   • determining which age group and clientele the activity would be most appropriate for
   • deciding whether it would be best used in an individual or group experience
   • explaining and demonstrating how they would use the tool to build connections with the student

4. Each student will present their object to the rest of the class, showing and explaining how the tool can be utilized to build connections with a child or adolescent and answering the previous questions. (10-minute presentation by each student)

5. After all students have presented their relationship-building tool, facilitate a large group discussion on the reactions and importance of the exercise. Encourage discussion on the importance of balancing between presenting problems of clients and building a relationship, particularly in the early stages of the counseling experience. Discuss the experience of presenting impromptu activities, the feelings that were encountered, and the role of a counselor to read, develop, and create a safe, comfortable place for a productive working alliance to grow. Encourage dialogue on the importance of flexibility and creativity in building the counseling relationship. (30 minutes)

Debrief questions:
1. How was this experience for you?
2. What are your reactions to others' presentations?
3. How is this relevant to your work with children and adolescents?
4. How does this relate to what we have learned about relationship-building strategies?
5. What is the importance of impromptu experience?
6. How might this experience support you in your professional role as a counselor?

Adaptations for other course formats:
This activity would be best used for in-person or synchronous online course format. For in-person courses, the students bring their items from home and are allowed some short preparation time before each student offers their presentation, concluding the experience with a discussion. For online synchronous courses, instructors ask students to find an object in their home and bring it to the class session, followed by the same format.

Exploring Spiritual Lifemaps in Counseling
(Buser et al., 2013)

Materials needed:
Blank sheets of paper or digital drawing tools (e.g., Canva, Jamboard)
Colored pencils, markers, or any drawing materials for in-person settings
A sample spiritual lifemap for reference (optional)
Prompts for reflection and instructions
Hodge's definition of spirituality and religion as a handout or slide

Time needed:
2+ hours

Learning objectives:
1. Enhance self-awareness by creating a personal spiritual lifemap or a lifemap of core life values.
2. Develop empathy and active listening skills by engaging in peer counseling sessions using the spiritual lifemap.
3. Reflect on the role of spirituality and values in counseling practice through experiential and written activities.
4. Increase comfort and competence in discussing spirituality, religion, and meaning with clients.

Instructions:
1. Introduce Hodge's (2005) definition of spirituality as "one's existential relationship with God (or perceived Transcendence) that fosters a sense of meaning, purpose, and mission in life" and religion as the outward manifestation of spiritual beliefs. Highlight the importance of using the client's own language and definitions when discussing spirituality and religion. Provide an overview of the spiritual lifemap, describing it as a strengths-based intervention to explore spiritually significant life events, coping strategies, and resources. (15–20 minutes)
2. Creating the spiritual lifemap. (30 minutes)

   • Distribute instructions for creating the spiritual lifemap.

- Students are given a blank sheet of paper and encouraged to sketch their spiritual/religious story using symbols, words, and a timeline format.
- Emphasize freedom of expression, noting that the map should reflect important rituals, turning points, or relationships that hold spiritual or personal significance.
- For students without a spiritual/religious focus, encourage them to map core values or life events that have shaped their sense of meaning and purpose.

3. Experiential counseling session. (30 minutes per round)

- Pair students and alternate roles:

  ○ *Client Role*: Share the spiritual lifemap, reflecting on its meaning, significant events, and personal strengths.
  ○ *Counselor Role*: Use open-ended questions to explore the lifemap, focusing on spiritual/religious strengths and resources. For example:

    ▪ How has your spirituality/religion helped you during challenging times?
    ▪ What role do rituals or spiritual relationships play in your life?

- Allow 15 minutes per role and then switch.

4. Facilitate a debrief where students share insights, challenges, or emotional responses from the activity. (10–15 minutes)

Debriefing questions:
1. How did creating the spiritual lifemap enhance your understanding of your own beliefs, values, or sense of meaning?
2. What insights or challenges arose during your counseling sessions?
3. How does the spiritual lifemap provide a strengths-based approach for exploring clients' spirituality/religion?
4. What considerations are important when using this tool with diverse clients?

Adaptation for other formats:

For online implementation, use digital tools like Zoom with breakout rooms for the counseling sessions. Lifemaps can be created using drawing apps or collaborative platforms like Google Jamboard. Reflection papers can be submitted through a learning management system, and group debriefing can be done via a synchronous virtual session or an asynchronous discussion board. This activity nurtures personal growth and equips students with practical skills for integrating spirituality and values into counseling in a sensitive and meaningful way.

Reference

Buser, J. K., Buser, T. J., & Peterson, C. H. (2013). Counselor training in the use of spiritual lifemaps: Creative interventions for depicting spiritual/religious stories. *Journal of Creativity in Mental Health*, 8(4), 363–380. https://10.1080/15401383.2013.844659

Rural Mental Health Display

(Crumb et al., 2020)

Materials needed:
Cameras or smartphones for taking photos.
Digital or physical space for displaying photos (e.g., Google Slides, physical boards, or shared folders).

Time needed:
Varies

Learning objectives:
1. Increase awareness of the unique aspects of rural mental health and living through photo elicitation.
2. Explore the roles of counselors and behavioral health professionals in rural settings.
3. Analyze and link lived experiences in rural communities to theoretical concepts, course content, and scholarly literature.
4. Reflect on strengths, challenges, and resources within rural communities to develop a deeper understanding of integrated behavioral health in these settings.

Instructions:
1. Provide an overview of photo-elicitation as a learning tool. Discuss its value in exploring social phenomena and fostering connections to lived experiences. Share examples of rural mental health themes (e.g., isolation, community strengths, healthcare access). (15–20 minutes)
2. Photo assignment instructions

   • Assign students to take three original photos that reflect aspects of rural mental health and rural living.
   • Explain the themes to consider:

      ○ Strengths and assets of rural communities (e.g., relationships, traditions).
      ○ Challenges and needs (e.g., stigma, access to care).

- Resources and strategies related to integrated behavioral health.

- Encourage creativity and diverse perspectives.

3. Photo analysis and caption writing (1–2 hours)

- Students write a brief caption (5–7 sentences) for each photo, addressing the following:

  - *Role of counselors or behavioral health professionals*: How does this photo illustrate challenges or opportunities in your role?
  - *Understanding of rural communities*: What insights does this photo provide into perceptions, strengths, assets, challenges, needs, or resources in rural communities?
  - *Integrated behavioral health*: How does this photo connect to the concept of integrated care in rural settings?

- Link each photo and caption to course concepts, textbook material, and at least one scholarly source.

4. Rural mental health display (30 minutes)

- Create a collective display of all photos:

  - *In-person*: Arrange printed photos and captions on a board or table for students to view.
  - *Online*: Use platforms like Google Slides, Padlet, or Jamboard to create a virtual gallery.

5. Facilitate a discussion based on students' displays (15–30 minutes)

Debriefing questions:
1. What themes emerged across the photos?
2. How did this activity deepen your understanding of rural mental health?
3. What unique challenges and strengths do rural communities face?
4. How might these insights inform your approach as a counselor or behavioral health professional?

5. What was the most surprising insight you gained about rural mental health through your photos or your classmates' displays?
6. How do rural strengths and challenges shape the role of mental health professionals?
7. What strategies might you employ to support mental health care in rural communities?

Reference

Crumb, L., Crowe, A., Dotson-Blake, K., & Flythe, A. (2020). Integrated behavioral health in rural settings: A course design. *Journal of Creativity in Mental Health*, *15*(2), 235–249.

Growing Together: Exploring Human Development through Nature

(Duffy et al., 2020)

Materials needed:
Journal or notebook (for reflections and sketches)
Pen, pencils, or colored markers (for sketching)
Camera or phone (optional for documenting nature)
Audio recorder or smartphone (for recording reflection on the solo excursion)
Research resources (internet access, books, or articles for plant research)
Access to natural outdoor spaces (e.g., water setting, wooded area, or student-chosen natural setting)

Learning objectives:
1. Explore the relationship between human development and nature, reflecting on how interactions with natural environments contribute to well-being.
2. Develop observational and reflection skills through the process of identifying and understanding the growth and development cycle of a plant in nature.
3. Analyze and present findings on the connections between nature, human growth, and counseling applications.

Instructions:

Part 1: water setting (instructor-guided)

1. Preparation: Before the excursion, assign *Last Child in the Woods* by Louv (2008) and provide prompts for students to reflect on.

   • Prompts:

     ◦ "What are your perceptions of Louv's premise that human needs interact with nature to develop in a healthy manner?"
     ◦ "What types of experiences have you had with nature that have shaped your reaction to this topic?"

- "What is it like to discuss this topic in an outdoor setting within the context of a human development course?"

2. Excursion: Take students to a water setting (e.g., river, lake, or pond). Encourage them to find a quiet spot to sit and reflect.
3. Reflection and Discussion: Allow time for personal reflection. Afterward, bring the group together for a group discussion to share their thoughts and insights. Engage in follow-up dialogue to help students make connections to the readings and the counseling applications.
4. Group Debrief: As a group, explore the idea of nature's role in human development and wellness and how this might relate to counseling practice.

Part 2: wooded area (instructor-guided)

1. Excursion: Take students to a wooded area. Ask each student to select a plant, observe it closely, and sketch it in their journal. They should focus on capturing the uniqueness of the plant's appearance.
2. Sensory Reflection: Have students write down words or phrases that come to mind as they observe, touch, and smell the plant. Encourage them to connect emotionally with the plant.
3. Research: Before the next class, students should research the plant, identifying its name, growth/development cycle, environmental needs, and challenges.
4. Class Presentation: In the next class, each student will present their findings, including their sketches, words/phrases, and the plant's life cycle. As students present, encourage them to draw parallels between the plant's growth and human development.
5. Group Discussion: Facilitate a discussion about the parallels between the plant's life cycle and human development, and how this understanding can be used in counseling practices.

Part 3: solo excursion (student-chosen)

1. Preparation: Ask students to choose a natural setting they feel drawn to (e.g., park, forest, beach, etc.). They will spend at least

30 minutes in the setting, paying attention to their five senses and emotional and cognitive states.

2. Reflection: Before leaving, students should either write, draw, or record their reflections about their experience in the setting. This should include their sensory perceptions, thoughts, and feelings.
3. Class Reflection: In the following class, have students share their reflections. Discuss how being in nature impacted their emotional and cognitive states and how these experiences can inform their work as counselors.

Debriefing questions:

1. What was your experience like on each of the three excursions? How did nature impact your thoughts, emotions, and senses during these activities?
2. How do the concepts discussed in *Last Child in the Woods* align with your personal experiences in nature?
3. How can understanding the life cycle of a plant help us understand human development in a counseling context?
4. How did being outdoors, in both a group and solo setting, influence your perception of wellness and human connection to nature?
5. How can these activities and reflections be integrated into your counseling practice? How might you use nature as a therapeutic tool with clients?

Adaptations for other course formats:

For students in an online setting, the nature-based excursions can be adapted using the following steps:

1. Virtual Nature Walks: If students cannot access outdoor settings, instructors can provide virtual tours of nature (e.g., YouTube videos of nature walks, scenic parks, or outdoor settings) for students to view. Students can still focus on the sensory and emotional experience while watching the video.

2. Solo Reflection: Students can still engage in the solo excursion by choosing a natural setting of their choice, but they can do so virtually by observing nature through digital platforms (e.g., websites featuring nature sounds, videos of forests, or time-lapse videos of plants).

3. Research and Reflection: Students can choose a plant from a virtual nature database or take part in a digital activity such as researching plant life cycles through online resources. They can submit sketches, reflections, and research findings online.

4. Online Discussion: Students can share their reflections and research findings in a virtual classroom setting (e.g., via video conferencing or discussion boards) and engage in group discussions about their experiences and insights.

In online environments, the emphasis will be on the reflections and the connection to the course material, with flexibility on how students engage with nature, either in-person or virtually.

Reference

Duffy, J. T., Springer, S., Delaney, M., & Luke, M. (2020). Eco-education: Integrating nature into counselor education. *Journal of Creativity in Mental Health, 15*(1), 55–68.

Theory Sale

Materials needed:
Various creative materials for poster presentations (stickers, markers, large paper, etc.)

Time needed:
90 minutes

Learning objectives:
1. Enhanced understanding of various counseling theories by synthesizing and presenting key concepts in a persuasive format.
2. Develop critical thinking and creativity by identifying unique strengths and practical applications of theory.
3. Improve collaboration and communication skills through group work.

Instructions:
1. Provide an overview of counseling theories that will be included in the activity. (5 minutes)
2. Randomly assign each group a theory. (2 minutes)
3. Each group works together to create a sales pitch for their assigned theory. (30 minutes)
4. Encourage creativity by allowing groups to design presentations to highlight theories' strengths, unique aspects, and practical applications. Groups should aim to convince their peers why their theory is the best choice for counseling practice.
5. Each group presents their sales pitch to the class. Encourage classmates to consider which theory they would buy and why. (40 minutes)

Debriefing questions:
1. What aspects of each theory stood out to you?
2. What did you learn about the strengths and practical applications of theory?

3. How did the presentations influence your perspective on counseling approaches?
4. What challenges did your group face in trying to sell your theory?

Adaptations for other course formats:

The activity can be easily conducted through virtual platforms for synchronous online courses. To boost engagement, incorporate polling tools that enable peers to vote on which theory they would choose. For asynchronous courses, the activity can be modified by having groups create video presentations or slide decks with voiceovers that showcase their sales pitch. A discussion board can function as a platform for students to ask questions, give feedback, and vote on their preferred theory. To enhance learning, students can be invited to reflect on their votes in a follow-up written post, explaining what they found compelling about the chosen theory and how it might apply to their future counseling practice.

Community Advocacy
(Chang, 2022)

Materials needed:
Art supplies (paint, markers, collage materials, poster boards, or digital art tools)
Access to multimedia tools for video or photography projects
Case studies or real-world examples of social justice issues in counseling
Ethical guidelines on advocacy and community engagement (ACA Advocacy Competencies, Multicultural and Social Justice Counseling Competencies)
Reflection journals or discussion boards for self-analysis

Time needed:
Varies

Learning objectives:
1. Develop social justice advocacy skills through experiential and creative engagement.
2. Apply the ACA Advocacy Competencies to real-world counseling and systemic issues.
3. Enhance self-awareness, cultural competence, and empowerment as future mental health professionals.

Instructions:
1. Begin with a discussion on why social justice advocacy is essential in counseling.
   Introduce various forms of advocacy, including client empowerment, public information, and systemic change. Discuss how creativity, through mediums like art, spoken word, film, and photography, can be a powerful tool for awareness, healing, and activism.
2. Students develop a project proposal that includes the social justice issue they are addressing (e.g., racial justice, LGBTQ+ rights, disability advocacy, destigmatizing mental illness, refugee experiences), the creative medium they will use (painting,

poetry, photography, music, documentary, social media campaign, storytelling, interactive art, etc.), and advocacy goals.

3.   Project development options:
Shortened Version (1–2 class sessions, 2–3 hours total):

• Students select an existing advocacy initiative and create a mini-project (e.g., a poster, infographic, or social media campaign).
• They present their work in a single class session or submit an advocacy reflection paper.

Moderate Version (2–4 weeks, integrated into coursework):

• Students develop a small-scale creative project (e.g., a poem, visual art, or spoken word performance) exploring a mental health or social justice issue.
• Reflection and discussion occur in weekly check-ins to track progress.
• The project is shared in a classroom gallery or virtual space.

Full-Term Project (6–10 weeks):

• Students engage in a full experiential advocacy process, including research, collaboration, project development, and community engagement.
• The project concludes with a public showcase or advocacy implementation beyond the classroom.

Debriefing questions:
1.   How did engaging in a creative advocacy project impact your understanding of social justice in counseling?
2.   What barriers or ethical concerns did you encounter in representing marginalized experiences?
3.   In what ways can counselors use art, storytelling, and activism to promote change?
4.   How do you see yourself continuing advocacy efforts beyond this project?
5.   How did this activity impact your self-awareness, cultural competence, and identity as a counselor?

Adaptations to other course formats:

For online adaptations of the advocacy and creativity project, students can present their work through a virtual art gallery using platforms like Google Slides, Padlet, or a dedicated course website to digitally showcase their projects. Discussion boards can serve as a space for students to upload their projects along with an advocacy statement, allowing for peer engagement and feedback. Additionally, students can create video presentations where they record short reflections explaining their projects and the impact they hope to achieve. Collaborative storytelling can be incorporated through tools like Flipgrid or Canva, enabling students to engage in interactive digital storytelling and advocacy work. A flexible timeline can be implemented to accommodate diverse learning needs, allowing students to complete their projects asynchronously over several weeks or in a more intensive short-term format, depending on course requirements.

Reference

Chang, V. (2022). Advocacy and creativity in community: A social justice project for counseling students. *Journal for Social Action in Counseling & Psychology, 14*(1), 2–16. https://doi.org/10.33043/JSACP.14.1.2-16

Experiential Group Work for Career Counseling
(Luke et al., 2022)

Materials needed:
Pre-designed career-related group activities or curriculum (e.g., career values exploration, privilege walk, career fears exercise)
Space for in-person group activities or virtual breakout rooms for online adaptations

Time needed:
Single-Class Activity (2–3 hours)
Weekly Group Series (4–6 weeks)

Learning objectives:
1. Increase student engagement in career counseling coursework by integrating experiential learning.
2. Help students explore their own career values, fears, and decision-making processes to enhance their empathy for future clients.
3. Apply career counseling theories in a practical, reflective setting.

Instructions:
1. Assign students to small groups (4–6 members) for peer-facilitated activity and discussion.
2. Assign one student to be co-facilitators who will lead the activity. The remaining students will participate as group members.
3. The facilitator will lead a career exploration activity and discussions.
4. Rotate peer facilitation roles to allow students to practice leading.

Debriefing questions:
1. How did engaging in an experiential group change your perception of career counseling?
2. What aspects of the group experience were most meaningful or challenging?

3. How might experiential groups help career counseling clients explore career concerns?
4. What insights did you gain about your own career journey and future counseling role?
5. How can you apply this group experience to your work with future clients?

Reference

Luke, C., Budesa, Z., & Diambra, J. (2022). Using an experiential group to promote engagement in a career counseling course. *Journal of Counselor Preparation and Supervision*, *15*(4). https://research.library.kutztown.edu/jcps/vol15/iss4/1

Counseling across the Lifespan
(Horton & Jacobs, 2023)

Materials needed:
Developmental stage-specific vignettes (included in the article)
Video clips from recommended media
Recorded role plays

Time needed:
20–25 minutes per developmental stage

Learning objectives:
1. Apply developmental theories to counseling practice across lifespan stages.
2. Practice culturally and developmentally responsive counseling strategies.
3. Explore emotional and ethical considerations in developmental counseling.

Instructions by developmental age:
1. Infancy (0–2 years):
    Focus: Supporting caregivers, postpartum mental health
    Materials: Clips from A Mouthful of Air (Koppelman, 2021)

    1. Show a film clip portraying Julie, a mother experiencing postpartum depression.
    2. Pair students. One plays Julie (client), and the other is the counselor.
    3. Conduct the first role play (5–7 minutes).
    4. Show a second clip focused on Ethan, Julie's husband.
    5. Have students switch roles and repeat the role play with the Ethan scenario.

2. Early childhood (2–6 years):
    Focus: Counseling caregivers of young children
    Materials: Vignette of Cassandra and Amari, parents of a 4-year-old (Horton & Jacob, 2023).

1. Read the vignette aloud or distribute it to students.
2. Set up a fishbowl: the instructor plays one parent, and a student plays the other.
3. Invite a student volunteer to act as counselor.
4. Begin the role play. Allow others to call "freeze" and take the counselor's place.
5. Continue the session with multiple volunteers, emphasizing developmentally appropriate parenting support.

3. Middle childhood (6–11 years):
   Focus: Emotional regulation, identity, family dynamics
   Materials: Clips from This Is Us and Turning Red

   1. Pair students with someone they don't know well.
   2. Show a clip of Randall from This Is Us dealing with racial identity.
   3. Assign roles: Student A is Randall (client), and Student B is the counselor.
   4. Role play (5–7 minutes), then switch roles.
   5. Show a clip from Turning Red showing Mei's struggles with puberty and family.
   6. Role play again with reversed roles.
   7. After both, students discuss their reactions and observations in pairs.

4. Adolescence (11–18 years)
   Focus: Identity exploration, gender, family values
   Materials: Recorded role plays (e.g., gender identity counseling, parent consult)

   1. Locate or record brief (10–15 minute) counseling role plays focusing on common concerns areas for adolescents.
   2. Pair students randomly.
   3. Play recorded role-play video (10–15 minutes).
   4. Instruct students to process quietly during the recording of immediate reactions, ideas, or emotional sessions as the session unfolds.
   5. Pause the video halfway for a quick partner reflection.

6. Resume the video and continue the same strategy.
7. After viewing, facilitate a debrief with questions:

    ○   What developmental issues stood out?
    ○   How did the counselor support identity and family dynamics?

5. Emerging adulthood (18–25 years)
    Focus: Trauma, identity development, military transition
    Materials: Nick vignette

    1. Group students into triads and number off 1–2–3.
    2. Role 1: Counselor | Role 2: Client (Nick) | Role 3: Observer.
    3. Begin the role play (5 minutes).
    4. Rotate roles clockwise until everyone has played all roles.
    5. Observers provide feedback after each round.
    6. After the triad completes all rounds, hold a small group discussion:

        ○   What developmental themes emerged?
        ○   How did trauma, identity, and emotion intersect?

6. Middle adulthood (25–65 years)
    Focus: Loss, identity redefinition, cultural values
    Materials: Lucia vignette

    1. Distribute or read the vignette aloud.
    2. In pairs, assign one student as Lucia (client) and the other as the counselor.
    3. Role play for 7–10 minutes.
    4. Switch roles and repeat.
    5. After both rounds, use these reflection prompts:

        ○   What psychosocial stage might Lucia be navigating?
        ○   How do her cultural background and grief experiences impact her counseling needs?
        ○   What came up for you personally or professionally?

7. Late adulthood (65+ years)
   Focus: Grief, depression, cultural values in aging
   Materials: Fatima vignette (shared only with "clients")

   1. Pair students and assign one to be the counselor.
   2. Pull all "clients" aside to review the vignette for Fatima.
   3. Instruct clients to begin the session by saying, "You're much younger than I expected."
   4. Conduct the role play for 7–10 minutes.
   5. Debrief with the whole class:
      ◦ How did you respond to unexpected client comments?
      ◦ What role did culture and grief play?
      ◦ How do developmental tasks differ at this stage?

Debriefing questions:
How did the developmental stage influence your counseling approach?
What challenges did you face in the role play?
How did culture, identity, or personal experience impact the session?
What ethical considerations emerged?
How does this stage connect to what we've learned about development theory?

References

Fogleman, D. (Creator). (2022). This is us [Television Series]. NBC.

Horton, E., & Jacobs, E. (2023). Practice makes progress: Using the lifespan course as an example for role-play implementation. *Journal of Counselor Preparation and Supervision, 17*(2), Article 3. https://research.library.kutztown.edu/jcps/vol17/iss2/5

Koppleman, A. (Director). (2021). A mouthful of air [Film]. Studio Mao.

Shi, D. (Director). (2022). Turning red [Film]. Pixar Animation Studios.

6

FOSTERING PROFESSIONAL DISPOSITIONS THROUGH CREATIVE APPROACHES

Developing professional dispositions is critical to counselor training, encompassing ethical awareness, self-reflection, interpersonal effectiveness, and cultural humility. Professional dispositions—such as openness to feedback, empathy, respect for diversity, and a commitment to ethical behavior—serve as the foundation for effective therapeutic relationships and responsible professional conduct.

This chapter explores how creative techniques can support cultivating these essential qualities in counselor trainees. Educators can deepen students' understanding of course content by integrating innovative activities and methods while fostering personal and professional growth. Each technique presented in this chapter includes a concise overview to guide its intentional use, a detailed list of required materials, step-by-step instructions for implementation, debriefing questions to facilitate reflection and discussion, and suggestions for adapting the activity to various learning environments, including online, hybrid, in-person, and residency programs.

Exploring Professional Dispositions

Carrie VanMeter, PhD, LPCC, LSC
Megan Mahon, PhD, LPCC-S

Material needed:
University Professional Dispositions and relevant ethical codes (i.e., ACA, ASCA, AMHCA, etc.)

Time needed:
1.5 to 2 hours

Learning objectives:
1. Demonstrate the ability to identify and analyze the professional dispositions outlined by their university, including recognizing behaviors and attitudes that align with or conflict with these expectations.
2. Create actionable solutions to address challenges related to professional dispositions and enhance their own or others' growth in these areas.
3. Articulate the supervisor's responsibilities in assessing and fostering professional dispositions, highlighting the collaborative nature of supervision in promoting ongoing professional development.

Instructions:
1. Create a Case Scenario: Begin by developing a case scenario focused on a supervisee struggling with professional dispositions during site-based learning (practicum or internship). This can be done either by the faculty or by the students. If specific issues need emphasis, it's advisable for the instructor to create the scenarios. Allowing students to generate scenarios provides insight into their understanding and concerns. (15 minutes)
2. Review the Case Scenario: Exchange or receive the case scenario. Students should read through it carefully to identify all relevant professional disposition issues. In group settings, students should discuss and ensure they have recognized all pertinent issues. (15 minutes)

3. Consult Guidelines and Rank the Professional Dispositions: After identifying the issues, students should first consult their university/program's professional dispositions and relevant ethical codes (e.g., ACA, ASCA, AMHCA, etc.). Next, they should rank the professional dispositions in order of importance and provide a rationale for their ranking. (10 minutes)

4. Develop a Supervisory Plan: Students should create a plan to address the professional dispositions identified in the scenario. This plan could include strategies for supervisors to approach conversations with supervisees, exercises for the supervisee, or resources to help improve the identified issues. (20 minutes)

5. Present the Plan: The final plan can be submitted in writing, presented orally, or delivered as a formal presentation, depending on the format chosen for the activity. (Dependent on format: 1 hour)

Debrief questions:

1. Why is it important for professional counselors to be aware of professional dispositions?

2. What were your initial reactions upon reading the scenario?

3. What challenges did you encounter while identifying and ranking the dispositions that the supervisee needs to work on?

4. What skills must the supervisor possess to effectively implement the proposed plan with the supervisee?

5. How can you assess your own professional dispositions?

6. What role do self-awareness and openness to feedback play in the development of professional dispositions?

Adaptations for other course formats:

This activity is highly adaptable and can be conducted in various formats. It can be done individually, in small groups, or as a whole class. If conducted virtually, you can utilize breakout rooms for group collaboration or presentations. In an in-person setting, the entire activity could be completed during class, or parts of it could be assigned as outside work if class time is limited. For an asynchronous course, the activity could be carried out through written exchanges or by organizing small groups that coordinate their meeting times. This flexibility ensures that the activity can be tailored to different instructional environments and time constraints.

Parable: Let the Rabbits Run

Xiaoxuan Qu, PhD
Melissa Luke, PhD, LMHC, NCC, ACS

Materials needed:
Let the Rabbits Run Parable (Clifton & Nelson, 1992)

Time needed:
30 minutes

Learning objectives:
1. Analyze personal beliefs and assumptions about education, learning, and student potential through critical engagement with the parable.
2. Reflect on how beliefs and practices impact diverse student populations, fostering awareness of cultural and individual differences in learning and growth.
3. Synthesize insights gained from the parable to inform the development of a school counseling vision and mission statement that reflects inclusivity, equity, and a commitment to student success.

Instructions:
1. Print out copies of the parable and distribute them in the classroom.
2. Ask each student to read a paragraph and continue reading in a circle until the reading is finished. (5–8 minutes)
3. After reading, show a list of processing questions (see below). (1–2 minutes)
4. Ask students to focus on one or two questions and share thoughts and feelings in relation to what they have made sense of the parable. (20 minutes)

Debrief questions:
1. What does education mean to you?
2. What does school counseling mean to you?
3. What does the little br'er rabbit need?

4. To what extent have various adults at the school provided services to meet the needs of the rabbit?

5. What general or specific thoughts do you have about the curriculum and education at large?

6. Think about your counseling work. In what ways will you know the needs of your (student) clients?

7. How would you choose to counsel children and adolescents in a culturally and contextually responsive way?

Adaptations for other course formats:
In addition to in-person learning, this parable can be used in a virtual classroom or assigned as an asynchronous assignment.

Reference

Clifton, D. O., & Nelson, P. (1992). Let the rabbits run: A parable. In D. O. Clifton & P. Nelson (Eds.), *Soar with your strengths*. A Dell Trade Paperback. Bantam Dell.

Self-Reflection with Group Sand Trays

Courtney Holmes, PhD, LPC, LMFT
Anne Catlett, LMFT, RPT-S, MBA

Materials needed:
Access to a wooden sand tray with sand is ideal. However, aluminum trays can be used with rice as a low-cost option with less mess
    A large and assorted collection of miniatures
    If doing this activity online, there is a free, public online sand tray application (https://onlinesandtray.com/)

Time needed:
30–90 minutes

Learning objectives:
1. Engage in self-reflection through the sand tray activity to better understand their role and relationships within themselves and with others, fostering a deeper awareness of their own experiences and emotions.
2. Understand how creative tools like the sand tray can supplement traditional counseling methods. Learn how to incorporate these modalities into their own therapeutic practices to support client expression and exploration.
3. Reflect on their individual roles and contributions within a larger system, gaining insight into how their presence and actions affect group dynamics and relationships.

Instructions:
1. This activity can be done in several ways; instructors can incorporate one or several options and adapt them to the class context. Given the class size, one might choose a large sand tray for the entire class and then break it up into small groups of three to five students. However, smaller class sections could use individual sand trays in addition to a group tray or as a stand-alone intervention.

Instructions for the large group sand tray:
1. Each student selects a figure that represents how they feel currently in graduate school
2. Each student describes their figure and why they chose it to the class
3. Each student places the figure in the sand tray
4. Students can view the collective sand tray

Instructions for the small group sand tray:
1. Each student can either select a new figure or use the one they selected for the large group tray
2. Together, the small groups create a sand tray that tells the story of their journey on becoming a counselor
3. Students present sand tray to the class

Instructions for an individual sand tray:
1. Each student can either select a new figure or use the one they selected for the large group tray
2. Each student creates a sand tray that tells the story of their journey on becoming a counselor
3. Students are invited to present sand tray to the class

Debrief questions:

Large group sand trays:

1. If this tray had a title, what would the title be?
2. If this group tray could talk, what would it say?
3. Who might like to share details about where their miniature is placed in the world and what you notice about where it is now after your peers have placed their miniatures in the tray?
4. How did this process feel to you?
5. What is something you learned about your peers through this process?
6. I wonder what makes this world safe or unsafe? What does it need to feel safer?
7. Tell me more about your process of working together to create this world.

Individual/small sand trays:

1. If this scene/world had a title, what would it be?
2. What was the process by which your group created this world?
3. Tell me more about the world you created.
4. I wonder what is happening in this world.
5. I wonder what happened before and what might happen after this scene.
6. If your miniature could talk, I wonder what it would say.
7. I wonder how the miniature you chose feels.
8. As you look at this world, what emotions do you experience?
9. I wonder how your body feels when you look at this world.

Adaptations for other course formats:

A synchronous online course may utilize this activity. Each student can complete an individual online sand tray and can be asked to screen share their final product with the class. Asynchronous courses could assign this task and have students share screenshots of their completed sand trays through the learning platform. Reflection questions could be answered in a class discussion thread or through private reflection assignments to the instructor. The online courses would not be able to utilize the group creation sand tray unless an application designed for shared, simultaneous cloud-based use was identified.

Creating Your Árbol de Fortalezas (Tree of Strengths)

Ana Ulloa Estrada, PhD
Nydia C. Sánchez, PhD
Claudia Alvarado-Sasse, MA

Materials needed:
Character Strengths Profile (Peterson & Seligman, 2004)
Link to Values in Action
Poster Board
Markers

Time needed:
1.5 to 2 hours

Learning objectives:
1. Reflect on their top three to five character strengths from the Values in Action (VIA) Character Strengths Survey and examine how these strengths shape their personal and professional identity as counselor trainees.
2. Explore the intersectionality of their strengths, considering how cultural, familial, and geographical factors influence their character strengths and how they can integrate these insights into their counseling practice.
3. Use the Árbol de Fortalezas (Tree of Strengths) activity to visually map and connect their personal strengths and growth areas to their counselor identity, fostering self-awareness and developing tools for resilience, self-care, and professional development in clinical practice.

Instructions:
1. Counselor trainees complete the Values in Action (VIA) online, which identifies their top three to five character strengths (signature strengths) and the bottom three to five character strengths (less utilized strengths).

2. Encourage trainees to take a few moments to reflect on major academic, personal, and cultural influences pivotal to their understanding of their character strengths.

3. Guide trainees in visualizing a tree that represents their cultural identity, journey, and strengths, such as a palm tree, cactus, oak tree, etc.

4. Provide various materials (poster board, markers, etc.) and space for students to draw their árbol de fortalezas (tree of strengths).

5. Instruct trainees that each part of the tree represents familiar and foundational experiences and influences on their personal and professional development.

6. The roots represent the sturdy base of the tree where signature strengths are revealed. This can include specific educational experiences, influential individuals, and familial or cultural experiences.

7. The trunk contains the top five signature strengths identified from the Values in Action (VIA) Character Strengths Survey. These are the core strengths that define trainees and guide their actions.

8. The branches symbolize their least utilized character strengths. These are the strengths that trainees might not often employ but have the potential for growth.

9. The leaves include strength-based activities or interventions that may emerge from trainees' least utilized strengths.

10. Flowers, fruits, or seeds (e.g., acorns, pinecones, etc.) represent the evolution of one's labor and the development of professional legacies. For instance, apples could represent the lessons learned from mentors, and lemons could symbolize hard-earned wisdom from life experiences. Cherry blossoms could reflect trainees' future-oriented contributions, such as innovative practices, programs, or policies, mentoring future counselors, or advancing equity and social justice in the field.

11. Encourage trainees to be creative in representing cultural contexts and meanings by adding symbols or animals.

12. Symbols may resonate with one's cultural context and personal meaning. For example, trainees might use a cross to represent

their religious identity, an emoji to represent joy, a yin-yang to symbolize balance, or a traffic light to indicate caution and mindfulness.

13. Animals may hold personal significance. For instance, a bird might symbolize freedom, a snail might represent patience, and a butterfly could denote transformation.

14. Facilitate a community-building circle where trainees are invited to share the different components of their árbol de fortalezas (tree of strengths). Encourage dialogue about how (a) signature strengths are central to trainees' professional identity, (b) potential growth areas are represented by least utilized strengths, and (c) trainees plan to integrate strength-based activities and interventions in their practice to promote diversity, equity, and inclusion

Debrief questions:

1. Creation Process (Opening Reflection): How did the process of creating your tree help you in understanding your journey, strengths, and areas for growth? What insights or realizations emerged during this creative process?

2. Roots (Foundation of Signature Strengths): What specific cultural or familial experiences do your roots represent? How have these experiences shaped your understanding of your core character strengths?

3. Trunk (Top Signature Strengths): How do your signature strengths help you navigate and bridge cultural differences in your clinical practice? Reflect on a specific example where you utilized one of your strengths to enhance intercultural understanding and communication.

4. Branches (Least Utilized Strengths): What are some areas of potential growth represented by the branches of your tree? How do you envision developing these less-utilized character strengths in your personal or professional life?

5. Leaves (Strength-Based Activities or Interventions): How do the leaves of your tree symbolize strength-based activities or interventions you might use in the future? In what ways can

these activities help you address diversity, equity, and inclusion in your counseling practice?

6. Flowers/Fruits/Seeds (Professional Legacy and Contributions): What do the fruits, flowers, or seeds on your tree represent about your evolving professional legacy? What contributions do you hope to make in the counseling field, and how do they reflect lessons you've learned from mentors or life experiences?

7. Cultural Symbols (Cultural Identity): What cultural symbols did you choose for your tree, and how do they represent key aspects of your cultural identity? How have these symbols influenced your approach to working with diverse populations?

8. Animals (Personal Significance): Did you include any animals in your tree? If so, what significance do they hold for you, and how do they connect to your journey of personal and professional development?

9. Overall Reflection (Integration and Growth): How do the different components of your tree come together to reflect your journey as a counselor trainee? In what ways will you integrate your strengths and areas of growth into your practice moving forward?

Special considerations:

Permit students to use various mediums (e.g., drawing, collage, digital art) to create their tree, accommodating different comfort levels and artistic abilities. Make sure that all materials and instructions are accessible to students with disabilities. Provide accommodations as needed, such as large print, digital formats, or assistive technologies.

Be aware of and sensitive to the diverse cultural backgrounds of the students. Use inclusive language that respects all cultural expressions and identities. Some cultural symbols or practices may have significant personal meanings that they might not want to disclose or explain to others. For example, students may also choose to include words in their native language or activist imagery.

Understand that some students may feel uncomfortable sharing their drawings due to personal, cultural, or emotional reasons. Emphasize that participation in sharing is voluntary. Consider offering students alternative ways to participate, such as sharing only specific parts of their tree or writing a reflective piece instead of presenting verbally.

Adaptations for other course formats:

The Árbol de Fortalezas activity can be adapted to any course format since the Values in Action (VIA) Character Strengths Survey is accessible online. In an online environment, instructors can refer students to create their drawing on Canva (or other tools like Google Slides or an online whiteboard). Then the debrief can be facilitated remotely on Zoom or through an asynchronous submission using the narration feature on Canva.

References

Estrada, A. U., & Haney, P. (1998). The use of multicultural genograms in family therapy. *Journal of Family Psychotherapy*, *9*(2), 55–62.

Institute on Character. (n.d.). *The VIA Character Strengths Survey.* https://www.viacharacter .org/account/register

Peterson, C., & Seligman, M. E. P. (2004). *Character strengths and virtues: A handbook and classification.* Oxford University Press and American Psychological Association.

Inside-Out: Mask-Making and the Counseling Student Identity

Jil Hus, PhD, LMHC(IN), NCC, ACS, BC-TMH

Materials needed:
Masks (paper-mâché, cardboard, or plastic)
Art mediums include but are not limited to markers, crayons, colored pencils, paint, and pastels
Various crafting supplies to decorate or craft the mask

Time needed:
2–2.5 hours

Learning objectives:
1. Engage in a creative mask-making process to reflect on their evolving professional identity as counselors, considering both their personal and professional selves and how these identities intersect and influence their counseling practice.
2. Use the artistic process of mask-making to express their personal and professional identities through symbolism, exploring how creative expression can deepen self-awareness and contribute to the development of their professional counselor identity.
3. Share their masks and the insights gained from the mask-making process with peers, engaging in group processing to deepen their understanding of self, gain diverse perspectives, and foster a supportive environment for the continued development of their counselor identity.

Instructions:
1. Provide students with the pre-questionnaire listed in the debriefing questions section. (30 minutes)
2. Students select masks. Ensure that individuals have access to numerous art mediums and materials and are free to select their preferences of items. (10 minutes)

3. Students are asked to consider the following prompt as they select their masks, mediums, and materials. How do you see yourself as a person? How do you see yourself as a counselor?

4. Students then complete their masks while considering the prompt and symbolism in the construction of their artwork. Symbolism can include but is not limited to the use of colors, symbols, shapes, words, designs, drawings, sketches, as well as anything else that comes to mind when considering the answers to the prompt above. (60–90 minutes)

5. Following mask completion, students will answer the post-questionnaire questions listed in the debriefing questions section. (30 minutes)

6. Once all masks and post-questionnaires are completed, regroup and allow individuals/members to go around and share (to their comfort level) the answers to the post-questionnaires while describing their masks and engaging in group processing. (30–40 minutes)

Debrief questions:

1. Participants are given a pre-activity questionnaire that contains the following:

   • Define professional identity in your own words.
   • What does it mean for you to be a counselor?
   • What thoughts and feelings have you experienced since beginning your field experience?
   • What does the term reflective practitioner mean to you?

2. Participants are given a post-activity questionnaire that contains the following:

   • Describe your thoughts and feelings during this experience.
   • Describe your masks, chosen mediums, and the reasons for items chosen.
   • Describe the metaphorical/symbolic content of your mask that speaks to both your personal and professional identities.
   • How does this activity provide reflection and insight into your developing professional identity and status in field experience?

Adaptations for other course formats:

Adaptations for asynchronous and/or virtual modalities would include finding printable/blank masks that can be emailed to individuals or screen-shared to allow individuals the ability to create and process choices of material selection and a mask that represents their shifting and integrating identities. Special considerations for this activity include ensuring all participants have access to masks, mediums, and materials, as well as offering alternatives for individuals with sensory sensitivities or physical limitations. The duration of the activity may vary depending on group size, course modality, and chosen materials, with the option to complete it in one session or across multiple sessions, allowing adequate time for both creation and group processing.

Reference

Hus, J. (2021). *Inside out: Mask-making and the counseling student identity* [Doctoral Dissertation, Walden University]. ProQuest Dissertations Publishing.

Using Expressive Arts in Group Supervision

Ajitha Chandrika Prasanna Kumaran, PhD, NCC, LPC

Materials needed:
Painting materials (watercolor, acrylic, pencil, eraser, crayons)
Paper/canvas
Stickers
Water or computer/laptop, Canva/Adobe

Time needed:
30 to 60 minutes

Learning objectives:
1. Use creative expression to explore and reflect on their counseling experiences, identifying key emotions, challenges, and growth areas encountered during their practicum or field placement.
2. Illustrate and analyze their relationship with their site supervisor through visual representation, fostering a deeper understanding of supervisory processes and how they impact their professional development.
3. Through group debriefing and sharing of their artwork, students will engage in collective reflection, gaining insights from their peers' experiences and enhancing critical thinking and problem-solving skills in the context of counselor training.

Instructions:
1. Instruct students to take what they need for the activity and settle down comfortably; they can use painting paper, a canvas, and any coloring tool they are comfortable using. (5 minutes)
2. Instruct the students that this activity is not to judge their painting or drawing skills; it is a processing activity for supervision. They will be given prompts and 20 to 30 minutes to illustrate their thoughts and feelings on the paper/canvas. If you want, you can choose more than one prompt. (30 minutes)
3. Students can draw, paint, or use symbols, emojis, or stickers to describe one of the prompts below:

- Illustrate your week in general.
- Illustrate your week as a counselor.
- Illustrate your supervision experience or relationship with your site supervisor.
- Illustrate your highs and lows with your clients this week.
- How are you feeling today or this week?
- Illustrate your expectations/concerns as a counselor this week/next week.

Debrief questions:
1. Tell us, what is happening in your paper or canvas?
2. How was this experience for you?
3. What are some things you learned from one another?

Adaptations for other course formats:
To utilize this activity in an asynchronous environment, educators can develop a collage discussion board or any other collage app or program. This can be completed in two parts.

Part 1

Students will create a collage using one of the following three prompts and post the collage on the discussion board. Students can use PowerPoint, Adobe, or Canvas to create the collage. Students will add a brief description of their collage in the discussion post. The description must contain a minimum of 20 sentences.

- Illustrate your supervision experience or relationship with your site supervisor.
- Illustrate your highs and lows with your clients this week.
- How are you feeling today or this week?

Part 2

Students will review and respond to other students' (minimum three) collage descriptions. While commenting, validate their experiences and add your comments to their experiences based on yours. Additionally, you can post follow-up questions to build the conversation on the discussion board.

Virtual Art-Making Round Robin

Traci Bitondo PhD, LPC, LPAT, ATR-BC, ACS, ATCS
Dan Summer PhD, LAC, ATR-BC, LPAT, LCAT, ATCS
Annette Vaccaro, EdD, LPAT, LPC, ATR-BC, ATCS, ACS

Materials needed:

Cloud-based collaborative drawing program (e.g., Draw.Chat [preferred], Excalidraw, Google Jamboard, Miro)
Computer, tablet, or phone for each student
Timer (digital or physical)
Printer for creating a physical book of the collaborative artwork (optional)
Journals or papers for reflection and self-awareness exercises

Time needed:

1 to 1.5 hours

Learning objectives:

1. Engage in a collaborative artmaking process to explore and express their emotions and experiences, fostering increased self awareness and emotional regulation essential for developing professional dispositions in counseling.
2. Cultivate empathy and refine their interpersonal skills by observing and contributing to each other's artwork, enhancing their ability to understand and respond to diverse perspectives and emotional states.
3. Engage in reflective practice by observing and modifying art created by peers, using this process to deepen their understanding of group dynamics, explore creative problem-solving, and integrate experiential learning into their counselor training.

Instructions:

1. Create a virtual "workspace" within the drawing program before the class starts, where each student has a blank page to start their artwork. Depending on the program used, different pages might be able to be created within the workspace, or separate workspaces might need to be created. Ensure you have links ready to share with students.

2. Number each page and assign a corresponding number to each student to help them recognize their starting point. Ensure all students can access each page before starting the activity. Provide time for students to become familiar with the art program. This will allow the instructor to assess any technical problems before starting. (5–10 minutes)

3. Art-Making Session: Instruct each student to start creating art on their designated page/space. Set a timer for 2–5 minutes, depending on class size and available time. When the timer goes off, have students move to the next page and continue adding to the artwork started by another student. Repeat this process until each student has contributed to every page and returned to their original piece. (20–40 minutes depending on class size)

4. Group Discussion and Debriefing: Review each piece of art collaboratively created by the class. Facilitate a discussion on the creative process, group dynamics, and any challenges faced during the activity. Encourage students to reflect on their thoughts about control, ideas, and feelings that emerged, and what it was like to collaborate with their classmates in this way.

Optional post-class activities:

1. Reflection and Journaling: Provide time for students to journal about their experience, focusing on self-awareness and reflexivity. Suggest prompts such as: "How did it feel to contribute to others' artwork?" "What did you learn about yourself through this process?" "What themes emerged?" "How is the art similar or dissimilar?"

2. Creating a Physical Book: Print each piece of artwork and compile them into a book. Distribute the book to students as a symbolic representation of their collective efforts, a means of continuing to reflect on the process and product, and a memento of the class experience.

Debrief questions:

1. How did you feel when adding to someone else's artwork?

2. What challenges did you encounter during the activity? Were there any surprises?

3. How did the time constraint impact your creative process?
4. What did you learn about group dynamics through this exercise?
5. How did this activity influence your understanding of control and perfectionism?
6. In what ways did the collaborative aspect of the activity impact your experience/learning?
7. How can the skills practiced in this activity be applied to your future counseling practice?
8. What insights did you gain about your own process?
9. What will you take away from this experience to use in other contexts?
10. What populations and settings are best for this activity? Are there any contraindications?

Adaptations for other course formats:
In an asynchronous format, students can be assigned to contribute to the artwork over a designated period, with scheduled check-ins for reflection on the creative process. Each student uses one color to ensure that their individual contributions are visually distinguishable when the artwork is completed. In an online synchronous setting, the activity can be facilitated using screen sharing and breakout rooms, allowing smaller group discussions during the debriefing session. This fosters deeper engagement and reflection. For an in-person version, students would use physical art materials to create their contributions, with artworks rotated among classmates in a classroom setting. The activity would culminate in a group discussion and debrief conducted face-to-face, providing an opportunity for shared reflection and connection.

Self-Care Tags

Annette Vaccaro, EdD, LPAT, LPC, ATR-BC, ATCS, ACS
Dan Summer PhD, LAC, ATR-BC, LPAT, LCAT, ATCS
Traci Bitondo PhD, LPC, LPAT, ATR-BC, ACS, ATCS

Materials needed:
Blank tags or small pieces of cardstock or artist trading cards
Markers, pens, or colored pencils
String or ribbon
Self-adhesive decorations (e.g., stickers, washi tape, collage materials)
Hole Punch
Optional: Laminating machine or laminating sheets

Time needed:
45–60 minutes

Learning objectives:
1. Engage in a creative process to identify and reflect on their personal self-care needs, increasing awareness of stress triggers and developing individualized strategies for managing well-being.
2. Creating personalized self-care tags, students will commit to integrating self-care practices into their daily routines, encouraging long-term habits that promote physical, emotional, and psychological well-being.
3. By participating in a group setting, students will acknowledge the importance of social support in self-care, recognizing their interdependence on others for maintaining overall well-being and fostering a sense of community.

Instructions:
1. Begin by discussing the importance of self-care for counselors and how it impacts their professional effectiveness and personal well-being. Next, discuss the utility of clothing care tags, asking students to think about the tags on their clothes and how these tags provide instructions for the best and recommended methods for taking care of that specific garment. Questions could

include: "Why is the clothing tag important?" "What are the dangers of not noting the tag or not following the recommendations on the tag?" Transition to the metaphor of creating a care tag for themselves, asking, "If you were to create a tag for yourself so you knew how to take care of yourself, what would you include?" "What do you require and what can be identified for optimal self-care for you?" The members should give as much detail as needed about the care to communicate to the reader about the proper care. (5 minutes)

2. Ask students to take a few minutes to reflect on their current self-care practices and consider what has been working for them, areas they may want to improve, or new strategies they want to implement. Encourage them to think about various aspects of self-care, including social, physical, emotional, mental, and spiritual practices. (10 minutes)

3. Provide each student with several blank tags or pieces of cardstock. If virtual, students will need instruction on creating a tag in advance of the activity. Generally, the tag is approximately 3 × 5 inches or longer. The tag should have a hole punched on one side, and a string or twine is threaded through the hole and tied for hanging later as a reminder. Instruct students to write self-care strategies on the tag. They can use markers, pens, colored pencils, or collage or scrapbook materials to decorate and personalize their tags. Optional: Students can laminate their tags for durability. (20 Minutes)

4. Students share their tags with a partner or in a small group, discussing why they chose each strategy and how they plan to incorporate it into their routine. The instructor will facilitate a brief discussion on the challenges of maintaining self-care and strategies for overcoming these obstacles. (10 minutes)

5. Encourage students to hang their tags in a visible place, such as on a bulletin board or string them together to create a banner. Conclude the activity with a reflection on the importance of self-care and how this activity can serve as a reminder to prioritize their well-being. (5 minutes)

Debrief questions:

1. What self-care strategies did you include on your tags, and why did you choose them?

2. What challenges do you face in maintaining consistent self-care practices, and how can you overcome these challenges?

3. How does self-care impact your effectiveness as a counselor?

4. How can creative activities like this one enhance your commitment to self-care?

5. What new self-care practices did you learn from your peers during the sharing session, and is there a new approach you want to try?

Adaptations for other course formats:

To adapt this activity to an asynchronous format, provide the students with a detailed written guide and a video demonstration that walks them through the process of creating self-care tags. After crafting their tags, they will engage in an online discussion board where they can share their creations and reflect on their self-care practices.

In a synchronous session, you can choose to have students create care tags using the traditional art supplies provided above, or you can give them the opportunity to use digital art tools. After completing their tags, students can be divided into breakout rooms, where they will discuss their self-care tags in small groups.

"Letting Go" and "Letting In" Creative Door Drawings

Kristin Erickson, PhD, LIMHP, LIPC, ACS, BCB

Materials needed:

Several sheets of blank paper (preferably in various colors). Cardstock works well, but not required

Items to draw with (include a variety of colors to choose from): Markers, Colored Pencils, Crayons, Oil Pastels, Pens, and Pencils

Time needed:

45—60 minutes

Learning objectives:

1. Explore and reflect on their personal and professional self-care practices by creating door drawings that symbolize what they wish to close the door to (unhealthy habits) and open the door to (healthy practices) in their lives.

2. Gain insight into using creative metaphors in therapy by applying the door drawing technique to help clients explore self care and well-being needs in a variety of settings.

3. Enhance their self-awareness through reflective engagement with the door drawing activity, identifying areas of growth and change in their self-care practices.

Instructions:

1. Before class starts, prepare the space by laying out a variety of paper and art drawing materials that the students can choose from for the door drawings. (5–10 minutes)

2. In class, when you're ready to begin the activity, start by giving an overview of the activity and explaining its purpose and potential benefits of using door drawings as metaphors for self-care. Clarify how creative interventions can encourage client self-reflection, growth, and development; help counselors connect with clients as they gain insights and engage in new ways of being, and support the personal growth and development of both counselors and those in training. (3–5 minutes)

3. Explain that the drawings of doors will serve as metaphors for their self-care and well-being needs. Invite students to explore their self-care challenges, "stuck points," growth edges, and identify what could help enhance their development or foster new ways of being. Two sheets of paper will be provided for each drawing. Remind students that their drawings don't need to be perfect, and they can always start over on a third sheet of paper if they wish. Some students may worry about "performing" or having "perfect" drawings; reassure them that they are not being judged for their work and encourage everyone to agree to create a judgment-free, safe space for drawing. Explain that students will turn to their neighbors to share their drawings when they are finished (and they can share to whatever degree they feel comfortable). (3–5 minutes)

4. Explain each drawing before the students do their drawings. (5–8 minutes, including discussion points below)

   Drawing No. 1. For the first drawing, students are to draw a closed door that is symbolic of things they would like to close the door on, or "let go" of, in their lives from a self-care and well-being perspective. Invite them to explore what no longer serves them, what they have been hoping to say "no" to in their lives, and/or what they feel "stuck-ness" with and/or might need closure to. A few additional points to share:

   • Students can draw their door however they would like. The door can be any shape and made of whatever material they would like—wood, brick, stone, water, grass, leaves, metal, a mirror, mist, fire, food, cloth, an ethereal medium, or a medium that doesn't exist yet. The door might have windows, bricks that are loose, holes in the door, bars or lock pads on the door. They are in charge of their choices and can draw their door however they would like.

   • Students can choose any time of day for their door (and a different time of day for either side of their door if they would like). It could be morning, midday, dawn, dusk, or deep into the middle of the night. They can also choose the location of the door and the size of the door. Whatever they do to remember the door serves as a symbolic metaphor for whatever it is they would like to let go of, close the door to, say goodbye to, say no to, or take a break from in their own life.

- Ask students as they draw to pay attention to what comes up for them pertaining to thoughts, feelings, and where they feel different parts of their drawing in their bodies.

Drawing No. 2. Explain that for their second drawing they will draw on a separate sheet of paper, an open door. This door does not have to be tied to or related in any way to their first drawing, but can be if they would like. This door is to be symbolic of what students would like to invite more of, keep open to, "let in," and/ or say "yes" to in their lives. Invite students to dig deep if they are comfortable doing so, and while drawing, really examine where they are at with self-care and how they are doing, what gets in the way, and what they feel they need at this time in their lives, whether real and tangible like people, experiences, hobbies, or relationships, or something internal, symbolic of hopes and dreams, rest, relaxation, or self-care related, and/or something more ethereal, mystical, spiritual, or superhero related. The sky is the limit.

- Explain that the same things apply to this door drawing; they can choose to draw the door however they would like and consider what the door is made of, the size and shape of the door, the time of day on both sides of the door, and what is on both sides of the door.
- Ask them, as they draw to again pay attention to what comes up for them pertaining to thoughts, feelings, and where they feel different parts of their drawing in their body.

5. Ask students if they have any questions. (2–3 minutes)
6. Have students choose their drawing materials to do their door drawings (i.e., start drawing). (10–12 minutes, including discussion points below)

- Invite the class to draw in a reflective meditative way, honoring silence as best as possible. This can help them go inward

and deeply reflect on what comes up for them as they draw. It also helps keep any interruptions to a minimum.
- Students who don't quite finish may complete them at home.
- If students finish early, they can sit quietly reflecting on their drawings and, on a separate sheet of paper, write a few paragraphs about each door drawing.

7. Next, students will turn to their neighbor and share what the process was like. Divide the time between the two students. Encourage students to share to what level they are comfortable sharing and pass on anything they are not comfortable sharing. Share: What jumped out to them? What it was like to try out a creative activity like this one? Did anything surprise them? How might this be similar to or different from traditional talk therapy interventions? Did their paper choice, medium choice, color choices, and door choice mean anything in particular to them? What was on either side of their doors, and did that mean anything in particular to them? What did they learn about themselves? What might they want to explore more after they leave today? (10–12 minutes)
8. Debrief the activity with students. Explore the experience, what they learned about themselves and their self-care needs, and what the next steps might be for them. Ask if there might be one or two people who would be willing to share their drawings. Explore how the activity could be easily adapted to use with clients. Explore ethical and multicultural considerations. (10 minutes)

Debrief questions:
1. What was the activity like to try out? What did you learn about yourself, and what insights did you gain that you might be comfortable sharing with us in this setting?
2. If you found this meaningful for you, how might the activity be continued or expanded upon for your own personal and/or professional development after leaving today?
3. How might this activity be adapted to use as a therapeutic intervention with clients? What clients and/or client issues might this not be the most helpful activity for?

4. What processing tips might you have for yourself when processing the activity with a client?

5. What ethical and/or multicultural considerations are important to keep in mind?

Helpful points to weave into the debriefing discussion:

- Remind students to avoid interpreting the drawings or judging any part of the drawings; invite the client role to interpret their own drawings.
- Also, remind students from an ethics perspective that they should avoid saying they are doing art therapy since they are not art therapists; art therapists have their own theories, credentials, and ways of implementing creative interventions using art.

Adaptations for other course formats:
If using this activity in an asynchronous course, you could make this an assignment.

- Explain the activity's purpose. Students will need to prepare for the activity; explain what art materials they will need for their drawings. Explain what they will be drawing, and as part of their assignment, they will upload a five-minute video reflection that shares how they are doing with their self-care, their drawings (what they are comfortable sharing), what jumped out at them, what insights they had, what they got out of the experience and learned about themselves, and how they might adapt an activity like this for use with clients, including cautions and considerations.
- Explain how students should record themselves (Zoom, YouTube, etc.) and when they are done, how they will turn in their assignment/upload the recording to whatever platform your program uses (Canvas, Blackboard, etc.).

Reflexivity Echoes

Frank Gorritz, PhD, LPC, NCC

Materials needed:

Materials can be recommended to students to accommodate diverse learning styles. For example, students can:

- Draw a circle and surrounding circles as the activity continues on a piece of paper. Students can use a game piece, token, etc., to place themselves in the circle, and then to expand to further circles as students engage in the activity.

Time needed:

30 minutes

Learning objectives:

1. Practice the skill of reflexivity to enhance their awareness of personal and cultural influences, fostering a deeper understanding of how their identities and social systems shape their perspectives and interactions with clients
2. Apply Reflexivity to Client Conceptualization
3. Integrate Reflexivity into Professional Practice

Instructions:

1. Ask students to center themselves in the best way that is familiar to them, whether that be grounding, deep breathing, meditation, etc. (1 minute)
2. Prompt the student to think about the following points and let them reflect and respond for at least *two to five minutes* before continuing with the next point listed below. (5 minutes)

   - What are the first thoughts that come to mind when conceptualizing your client?
   - What kind of message do you feel these thoughts are conveying to you as they echo in your mind?
   - Where do you feel these thoughts came from when thinking about your life and lived experience?

- What social identities do you carry and how does this influence your thinking about a client? Try to think about how your identities such as race, gender, sexuality, ability status, ethnicity, etc. may be influencing the echo of thought that conceptualizes your client.

3. Check in with the students regarding how they are feeling and/or where their thoughts and echoes about the client are leading them in counseling work: Is there discomfort? Are there questions you have regarding things you want to know about your client's life?

4. Prompt the students to think about the following points and let the counselor-in-training reflect and respond for at least *two to five minutes* before continuing with the next point listed below:

   - What are the first thoughts that come to mind when conceptualizing your client now?
   - What social identities does your client carry and how may this influence how they are feeling? The point here is not to assume, yet to imagine as part of forming an empathic connection with a client who can feel othered in certain social contexts.
   - What types of echoes in their mind may they be experiencing? How do these echoes make you feel if you can reflect on that for a minute?
   - How can you use today's echoes and reflections to ensure your client's actual echoes feel heard and understood by you?

5. Debrief as needed depending on the insights that come forward from this activity.

Debrief questions:
1. What did you learn about yourself and how your cultural identities can show up in counseling?
2. If your client knew the echoes you experienced today, how do you feel your experienced echoes can impact the client(s) you conceptualized today?
3. How can you make note of the echoes you experienced today to make further sense of them and how they influence your experiences?

4. As you think about the echoes you experienced today, what types of resources can guide your learning and curiosity about different social identities from your own? (Guide and support counselors-in-training as needed depending on their developmental level.)

5. Outside of sessions, how can you make further effort in connecting with the actual narratives of clients who may differ from you in social identity?

6. How can you use what we did today to listen to the echoes of your mind for a minute as you continue to work with clients, especially with clients who may be different from you?

Debrief questions (if working in groups):

1. Did you notice any similarities or significant differences between the echoes that came from your peers today? Let's discuss and process if you feel comfortable sharing.

2. What can you learn from the echoes you experienced today to build a stronger connection with classmates who are different from you?

3. If you feel comfortable sharing, how do you feel that hearing the echoes of others around you impacted you during today's activity?

Special Considerations

It is important to note that the dialogue that can emerge from this activity can hold very sensitive meanings for the counselors-in-training you may be working with, as well as yourself when you hear the echoes of others you may be working with as a counselor educator. Make sure to hold space for students to share their thoughts and feelings with you as they continue to experience and process transformative insights as counselors-in-training.

When using this activity in groups, make sure to set group norms to ensure respect between classmates (e.g., no interrupting, no targeted comments toward another classmate during the activity, etc.). Counselor educators will also want to reflect on shared norms that communicate respect, support, and non-judgmental atmospheres in learning spaces if this is going to be a group activity with multiple students.

Adaptations for other course formats:

Other than the special considerations mentioned for using this activity with groups of students, there are no significant adaptations that need to be made for multiple formats. However, if using this activity with a group of students, ensure that enough time is provided for groups of students to process the prompts and debriefing that follows. When using with groups, it is recommended that the activity lasts for at least one hour for adequate reflection and insight building among students.

Capturing Insights: Using Photography to Enhance Development of Self, Professional Identity, and Multicultural Awareness

(Schmidt et al., 2019)

Materials needed:

Smartphones, tablets, or cameras (paired students can share devices if needed)

Access to a chosen setting (e.g., campus, local area, or personal space)

Writing tools or note-taking apps for reflections and narratives

A projector or screen for displaying photos during group discussion (for in-person settings)

Online platforms for sharing photos and reflections (e.g., Padlet, Google Slides, or a learning management system)

Time needed:

60–120 depending on the chosen assignment

Learning objectives:
1. Encourage creative exploration of emotions and perspectives to deepen self-awareness and empathy.
2. Help students connect personal emotional experiences with professional competencies in counseling.
3. Facilitate understanding of how diverse perspectives influence interpretation and interactions.
4. Promote dialogue on inclusivity, accessibility, and the sociopolitical context of counseling environments.

Instructions:
1. Introduce the activity. (10 minutes)

   - Explain the purpose of using photography to explore emotions and perspectives.
   - Discuss safety, cultural, and environmental considerations.
   - **Provide Assignment Options:**

- Offer students a choice of the following photography activities:

    a. **Capturing Emotions:** Photograph objects/scenes representing a challenging emotion.
    b. **New Perspectives:** Take images of a familiar object from varied angles to explore it differently.
    c. **Through Different Lenses:** Assume a specific role (e.g., client, caregiver) and photograph a relevant environment from that perspective.
    d. **Viewfinder:** Document their perception of their community and write accompanying narratives.

2. Activity. (60–90 minutes)

    - Students select their assignment and complete it independently or with a partner.
    - For partnered activities, ensure each participant takes turns sharing devices and perspectives.

3. Reflection. (15–20 minutes)

    - Students select one to three photos to share and write a short reflection (one to three paragraphs) about their experience and insights.

Debriefing questions:
1. For "Capturing Emotions":

    - What emotion did you choose to represent, and why?
    - How does this emotion challenge you personally and professionally?
    - What did you learn about creating space for challenging emotions in counseling?

2. For "New Perspectives":

    - What surprised you about the object after exploring it differently?
    - How does this apply to shifting perspectives in therapeutic work?

3. For "Through Different Lenses":

   - What insights did you gain from the perspective you adopted?
   - How can this exercise improve your empathy for clients?

4. For "Viewfinder":

   - What themes or messages emerged from your photos?
   - How do these reflect your view of your community and its challenges?

Adaptations for other formats:

1. Photo Sharing: Students upload photos and reflections to a shared online platform (e.g., Padlet, Google Drive). Use break-out rooms for small-group sharing and discussion.
2. Facilitated Discussion: Host a live virtual discussion or create a discussion board for students to comment on each other's work.
3. Narrative Submissions: Students submit reflections and photos as a portfolio to be reviewed and discussed asynchronously.

Reference

Schmidt, M. K., Murdock Bishop, J. L., & Becker, K. (2019). Using photography to enhance development of self, professional identity, and multicultural awareness. *Journal of Creativity in Mental Health, 14*(1), 105–114.

Leaves of Connection

Ashley Davis, PhD, LPC/MHSP (TN), ACS, NCC

Materials needed:
Post-it notes (various colors are preferred but not required)
Large flip chart pad or dry erase board
Marker
Pens/pencils

Time needed:
45 minutes

Learning objectives:
1. Identify and articulate personal concerns, questions, and anticipations related to the learning experience or transition into residency, fostering self-awareness and emotional expression.
2. Demonstrate group cohesion and shared experience by recognizing common themes among peers' responses, promoting empathy and mutual support within the learning community.
3. Reflect on changes in emotional state (e.g., anxiety or excitement) through group discussion and visual engagement, enhancing students' ability to process and regulate emotions in a supportive setting.

Instructions:
1. Draw a tree (trunk and branches only) on the large flip chart page or dry-erase board.
2. Pass out various colors of Post-it notes to students. Give them three to four each. Students can use more or less, if they wish.
3. Ask students to write down things they are nervous about, questions they have, or things they are looking forward to. I let students know that they can also write down things that they are nervous about that are outside the classroom (i.e., leaving their jobs, family, pets, etc. during residency).

4. Students are asked to put their post-it notes on the tree to represent leaves.

5. Once students have finished, the instructor reads them off one by one. The instructor answers the questions that are posted, validates the anxiety, and helps to join the group by pointing out commonalities.

6. The students and instructor debrief the activity.

Debriefing questions:

1. What are your thoughts/takeaways from this activity?
2. How has your anxiety level changed from the beginning of this activity?
3. What was it like to see so many similar responses?
4. What do you still have after completing this activity?
5. What support do you need from the group?
6. How has your excitement level changed from the beginning of the activity?

Adaptations for other course formats:

This activity can be adapted to be a synchronous virtual activity. Using a platform such as Google Jamboard allows participants to add their "leaves" to a virtual whiteboard.

Creating Your Superhero Values Cape

Materials needed:
Personal Values Card Sort (Miller et al., 2001)
Various crafting supplies to create the cape

Time needed:
1.5 to 2 hours

Learning objectives:
1. Examine the Influence of Core Values on Counseling Practice.
2. Develop Self-Awareness of Biases and Assumptions.
3. Integrate Personal Values into Counselor Identity.

Instructions:
1. Give each student a set of value cards and explain the task of ranking these values based on their significance. Make sure to emphasize that there are no right or wrong answers. (5 minutes)
2. Instruct students to sort the cards into three categories: Most Important, Important, and Least Important. While they are sorting, you may want to reflect on their experiences, things you notice, and debriefing questions. (15 minutes)
3. After their initial sort, have students narrow down their top five to ten values. (10 minutes)
4. Have students think about how they can visually represent their top values on the cape. Provide various materials (pens, markers, stickers, paper, etc.) and space for students to design and create superhero capes. Encourage them to be creative—use symbols, words, colors, and images that resonate with the values. (20 minutes)
5. Place students into small groups to explain their capes' elements and what they represent. (15–20 minutes)
6. Facilitate a large group discussion on how these values will impact their development and practice as counselors. Encourage dialogue on how their values might play out in real counseling scenarios. (20–30 minutes)

Debrief questions:

1. How do your identified values align with your chosen career path as a counselor?
2. Are there specific values that you believe are particularly relevant to your future profession?
3. How might your values impact your relationships with clients in a counseling setting?
4. Were there any cultural or diversity-related aspects that influenced your values sort?
5. What strategies could you use when your values conflict with a client's?
6. How do you plan to navigate potential value conflicts in your counseling practice?
7. How might your values positively contribute to your effectiveness as a counselor?
8. How might reflecting on your values enhance your ongoing professional development?

Adaptations for other course formats:

This activity can be adapted to any course format. For online use, instructors can distribute the value cards sort to students before class or create an online form where students can rank the values.

In a synchronous online environment, instructors can use breakout rooms for small group discussions, polling, and chat features to gather quick responses. Students can collaborate in real-time to design their capes using tools like Google Slides or an online whiteboard. In an asynchronous environment, students can upload their capes to a shared class gallery or discussion board and explain their values in writing or video.

Regardless of the format, encourage active participation through polls, breakout room discussions, and peer feedback. Ensure students are comfortable with the digital tools being used and offer support or tutorials as needed.

Reference

Miller, W. R., C'de Baca, J., Matthews, D. B., & Wilbourne, P. L. (2001). *Personal values card sort.* University of New Mexico. https://www.guilford.com/add/miller11_old/pers _val.pdf?t=1

Ethical Fairy Tales: Exploring Ethical Dilemmas through Storytelling

(Henderson & Malone, 2012)

Materials needed:
Copies of adapted fairy tale case studies (Henderson & Malone, 2012)
American Counseling Association (ACA) Code of Ethics (2014)
Ethical decision-making model framework
Whiteboard or virtual collaborative document (for group discussions)

Time needed:
60–90 minutes

Learning objectives:
1. Apply the ACA Code of Ethics to analyze ethical dilemmas in counseling practice.
2. Utilize ethical decision-making models to navigate ethical complexities.
3. Develop critical thinking and problem-solving skills in ethical scenarios.
4. Increase awareness of power dynamics, relational ethics, and cultural considerations in counseling.
5. Engage in collaborative ethical reasoning to explore multiple perspectives on ethical dilemmas.

Instructions:
1. Begin by reviewing the importance of ethics in counselor education. Discuss the ACA Code of Ethics (2014) and the role of ethical decision-making models. Explain the relational-cultural perspective, which emphasizes power, mutual empathy, and authenticity in ethical decision-making.
2. Divide students into small groups and assign each group an ethical fairy tale case study found in Henderson & Malone, 2012. Each group will identify the ethical dilemma in the case, apply relevant ACA ethical standards to the scenario, create an ethical

decision-making model to analyze potential solutions, and consider cultural, relational, and power dynamics influencing the ethical decision.

Little Bo Peep (Bartering in Counseling)
Cinderella (Subpoena & Confidentiality)
Snow White (Duty to Warn & Protect)
Rapunzel (Boundary Issues & Dual Relationships)
Little Red Riding Hood (Mandated Reporting & Confidentiality with Minors)
The Little Mermaid (Client Autonomy & Multiple Roles in Counseling)

3. Each group presents its case study, ethical dilemma, and proposed resolution.

Engage in whole-class discussion, comparing different perspectives and ethical interpretations.

Use the whiteboard or virtual document to map out ethical decision-making considerations.

Debriefing questions:
1. How did analyzing ethical dilemmas through fairy tales impact your understanding of ethical decision-making?
2. What challenges did you face in applying ethical standards to ambiguous situations?
3. How do power dynamics and relational factors influence ethical choices in counseling?
4. In what ways did your group's discussion change or challenge your initial assumptions about the case?
5. How can creative approaches, like fairy tales, enhance ethical reasoning in counselor education?

Adaptations for other course formats:
To adapt this activity for online courses, instructors can utilize virtual group work by assigning students to breakout rooms in Zoom for small-group discussions on ethical dilemmas. Collaborative documents, such as Google Docs or shared discussion boards, can be used for students to

annotate and analyze fairy tale case studies together. To deepen engage-ment, a discussion board reflection component can be incorporated, where students post their thoughts on ethical dilemmas and provide peer feedback. Additionally, instead of using traditional fairy tales, instruc-tors can implement a video case analysis by assigning students to analyze ethical dilemmas depicted in films or TV shows, encouraging them to apply ethical principles to real-world scenarios.

Reference

Henderson, K. L., & Malone, S. L. (2012). Ethical fairy tales: Using fairy tales as illustrative ethical dilemmas with counseling students. *Journal of Creativity in Mental Health*, 7(1), 64–82.

Vision Boards for Counselor Development
(Tipton et al., 2024)

Materials needed:
Magazines, newspapers, or printed images
Scissors, glue, and poster boards (or digital collage tools)
Markers, stickers, or any additional decorative materials

Time needed:
60–90 minutes

Learning objectives:
1. Enhance self-reflection and insight into professional identity development, values, and career aspirations.
2. Apply the Integrative Developmental Model (IDM) to understand developmental tasks and challenges faced by early-stage counselors.
3. Utilize vision boards as a creative supervision tool to externalize goals, strengths, and areas for growth.

Instructions:
1. Begin with a discussion on the challenges of early-stage counselor development, including self-doubt, perfectionism, anxiety, and struggles with autonomy. Introduce the Integrative Developmental Model (IDM) and explain how early-stage counselors often experience high motivation but also high anxiety and self-doubt (Stoltenberg & McNeil, 2009).
2. Provide students with magazines, newspapers, printed words, and images (or access to digital collage tools for online participation). Ask students to choose images, words, and symbols that represent their:

   Current identity as a counselor-in-training (strengths, personal values, skills they bring to the field)
   Challenges or barriers they face in their development (perfectionism, self-doubt, fear of failure, wellness concerns)

Aspirations for their future career (theoretical orientations, ideal work settings, professional goals)

3. Students arrange their selections on a poster board or digital canvas, visually representing their counseling journey. Encourage students to incorporate personal affirmations or motivational quotes that resonate with their professional growth.

4. In small groups, students present their vision boards, explaining the significance of the images and words they chose and what aspects of their professional identity are emerging.

   What they hope to develop further in their training. Facilitate a group discussion on common themes and struggles among early-stage counselors.

Debriefing questions:

1. How did creating the vision board help you understand your professional identity as a counselor?

2. What challenges surfaced as you worked on the vision board, and how do they relate to your development?

3. How did externalizing your goals and fears through a visual medium impact your self-awareness?

4. How can vision boards be integrated into supervision and self-reflection practices?

5. What steps will you take to revisit and refine your vision as you continue training?

Adaptations for other course formats:

In the online adaptation of the vision board activity, students can create digital vision boards using online tools. They will then upload their completed boards to an online discussion board, where they must provide written reflections on their work asynchronously. Additionally, virtual small group discussions will be facilitated through Zoom breakout rooms, allowing students to share and discuss their boards in real time. To ensure continuous growth and self-assessment, students will be encouraged to periodically update their digital vision boards and track their progress.

References

Stoltenberg, C. D., & McNeill, B. W. (2009). *IDM supervision: An integrative developmental model for supervising counselors and therapists* (3rd ed.). Routledge.

Tipton, J. L., White, D., Kim, H., Anderson Walker, S. B., & Diambra, J. (2024). Using vision boards to support the development of early student counselors. *Journal of Creativity in Mental Health, 20*, 1–16. https://doi.org/10.1080/15401383.2024.2369073

Reflect to Connect
(Trottier, 2024)

Materials needed:
A structured experiential learning activity like any within this book
PEARLS Debriefing Cognitive Aid (available at debrief2learn.org)

Time needed:
60–90 minutes

Learning objectives:
1. Identify their initial emotional and cognitive reactions to an experiential activity.
2. Analyze their performance using self-assessment, focused facilitation, and peer feedback strategies.
3. Engage in and reflect upon a psychologically safe and culturally responsive debriefing process.

Instructions:
1. Engage the class in an experiential activity and identify how you will utilize the Promoting Excellence and Reflective Learning in Simulation (PEARLS) framework (Eppich & Cheng, 2015).
2. Begin the debriefing process by explaining its purpose. Emphasize confidentiality, emotional safety, and the five stages of the debriefing process. Sample prompt: "Now that we've completed our activity, we'll spend about 30–45 minutes reflecting using the PEARLS framework. This space is meant to be supportive and collaborative—your insights and feedback are valued."
3. Start the reaction phase by prompting students to share their initial emotional responses. Guide them back to affective states if they bypass feelings. Sample prompt: "What were your immediate reactions or feelings during the activity?"
4. Move to the description phase, where you engage students in co-constructing a factual narrative of what occurred. Sample prompt: "Can you describe what happened during the session? What did you observe?"

5. The next stage is where most of the learning happens. The analysis phase assists students in transitioning from describing what occurred to making sense of why it happened and how it relates to their growth as students (Eppich & Cheng, 2015; Trottier, 2025). The following are key components:

   • Encourage students to focus on their strengths and contributing factors rather than surface-level answers. This can be done through discussion, journaling, or peer questioning. A sample prompt is "What are you most proud of in your performance?" "What specific choices felt intentional or aligned with your counseling identity?" "What would you modify or improve if you were to do this again?" "What theoretical or personal lens were you drawing from?"
   • If any key learning objectives were not met, guide students to greater insight through a use of observation and curiosity. A sample prompt is "I noticed you shifted topics when the client became upset. I wonder if you were trying to protect the client—or maybe yourself- from distress. What might be going on for you in that moment?"
   • Encourage learners to offer one another feedback using the same format of observation and curiosity. A sample prompt is, "How did your partner's choices affect your experience in the role play?" "What did you notice about their use of microskills that could be applied to your practice?"
   • If needed, provide feedback or additional teaching when students struggle to self-identify a performance gap. Always aim to clarify rather than correct.

6. Lastly, wrap up with experience by looking into future applications and personal takeaways. This assists students in consolidating insights and considering how they may use these in the future. This can be done verbally or in written summaries; however, consider integrating creative strategies. Example integrations:

   a. Each student shares one word or metaphor that captures their main takeaways. This can be written on a virtual whiteboard or sticky notes.

b. Invite students to draw a quick sketch or find a symbolic image of what they are taking away from the debriefing.

c. Ask students to write a short letter to themselves as if it were some time in the future. They should include what they learned and how they plan to apply it.

d. Students write one actionable goal on a card or journal page that spirals forward from today's experience. This might include a new technique they want to practice or a reflective question they want to explore.

Debriefing questions:

1. How did it feel to engage in the debriefing process using this structure?

2. What helped or hindered your ability to reflect deeply?

3. What did you learn about your counseling style or decision-making?

4. How did the group environment affect your comfort with sharing?

5. What will you carry forward into future practice?

Adaptations for other course formats:

In synchronous in-person or virtual classrooms, the PEARLS debriefing process can be facilitated in real time, with the educator guiding each phase and incorporating small group discussions or breakout rooms to enhance engagement. For asynchronous courses, adaptations involve shifting the debriefing process into written or recorded formats. Students can complete guided debriefing prompts through journal entries, discussion board posts, or video reflections using tools. Each phase of the PEARLS model can be scaffolded across modules—for example, one module may focus on reactions and description, while the next invites analysis and application. In these asynchronous settings, instructors can offer feedback through written comments or video responses to sustain dialogue and promote connection. For courses emphasizing clinical skills, asynchronous learners can record mock sessions and use the PEARLS framework to self-assess or exchange structured feedback with peers, creating a reflective dialogue outside real-time interaction.

These adaptations maintain the integrity of the reflective process while meeting the diverse learning needs of students in varied instructional formats.

References

Eppich, W., & Cheng, A. (2015). Promoting Excellence and Reflective Learning in Simulation (PEARLS): Development and rationale for a blended approach to health care simulation debriefing. *Simulation in Healthcare*, *10*(2), 106–115. https://doi-org .library.capella.edu/10.1097/SIH.0000000000000072

Trottier, D. G. (2024). Debriefing experiential learning in counselor education. *Counselor Education and Supervision*, *63*(2), 145–160. https://doi.org/10.1002/ceas.12299

APPENDIX A

CONFIDENTIALITY AGREEMENT

Establishing trust in the helping relationship and providing a safe place for personal disclosure are hallmarks of the helping professions. These characteristics are facilitated by the ethical practice of maintaining confidentiality within the helping relationship, and part of your professional development is learning to respect what is disclosed by others. Throughout this course, personal information may be shared; therefore, learning to maintain confidentiality is essential.

By signing this form, you agree to uphold the confidentiality of your fellow students' personal disclosures. While you may discuss the general activities of the class with others, it is strictly prohibited to reveal any personal information shared by classmates to anyone outside this class. Additionally, discussing another student's disclosures with classmates who were not present during the original session would be inappropriate.

It is important to recognize, however, that confidentiality has limitations. In situations where there is a concern for physical safety or well-being, it is your responsibility to inform the instructor. The instructor will assess whether any further action, including formal reporting, is necessary to ensure the safety and best interests of the individual involved.

Class Guidelines

- Personal information shared in the class is the property of the class and is not to be taken outside of this context.
- Engage in respectful discussions, even when opinions differ. Personal attacks or dismissive comments are not permitted.

- If any activity or discussion becomes personally challenging, students are encouraged to take a step back, notify the instructor as needed, and practice self-care. Participation is important but not at the expense of personal well-being.
- Fully attend to the person sharing. Listen with your ears, observe with your eyes, pay attention to what you are feeling, and reflect on your reactions.
- Use "I" statements when giving feedback. Be concrete, specific, and objective.
- You get out of this class what you put into it. Come prepared for each class by completing readings and assignments ahead of time.
- Limit the use of laptops, tablets, and phones to note-taking or research related to class activities. Refrain from unrelated activities (e.g., texting, browsing social media) during class.
- If you choose to raise a personal issue that leads to a strong emotional reaction, your instructor may refer you to counseling services outside of the context of the class.
- Throughout the course, students are encouraged to reflect on their experiences and provide feedback. Regular feedback sessions create an open dialogue and allow adjustments to be made as needed.

I agree to the conditions stated above.

_____   _____

APPENDIX B

STUDENT HANDOUT

The Tale of the New Flight Attendant:
An Informed Consent Activity

Imagine you are taking a trip somewhere, and to get there, you must take a plane. You have never flown before and are feeling some anxiety about it, as well as some excitement. As you board the plane and walk past the crew area to find your seat, you notice a flight attendant frantically flipping through a pamphlet with the title: "Keeping Passengers Safe: 101." You see that step 1 listed on the pamphlet is "How to use an oxygen mask" and step 2 is "How to use your seat cushion as a flotation device." Meanwhile, the flight attendant is so busy with the pamphlet that they do not seem to see you, much less welcome you onto the airplane.

When the plane doors close for departure, the flight attendant gets on the microphone to make a safety announcement. They hold a microphone in one hand, the pamphlet in the other, and—making no eye contact—begin to speak:

"Um, let's see here...hold on a second, let me look through my pamphlet. This is my first day, everybody. Can you tell? Okay, here we go: oh yeah, oxygen! If you need oxygen, there's a thing that comes down, like a mask, but I'm not exactly sure how that works. Hold on just a sec, where is it? Well, anyway, we probably won't need it, but if we do, just look around. You're smart; you can figure it out.

Oh, yeah—there's other important safety stuff you should probably know, but just look at the card in the seat pocket. It says grab a...oh, what is it called again? A floaty thingy? A flotation device, I think. You can read it all there or look at the pictures and figure it out. No big deal. It's pretty boring stuff, but you know, we have to cover it just in case there's a fluke accident, which never really happens anyway.

Time to take off now, so I'll wrap this up. It's all standard stuff, so I'm sure you don't have any questions, right? I didn't think so. Let's get on with the flight!"

Assignment:

Part 1. After reading through the story, consider these questions:

- What attitude does the flight attendant convey about the safety material? Do you get the sense that they see it as important?
- How safe would you feel with this flight attendant?
- Would you feel fully prepared to act on their safety information in an emergency?
- Would you want to continue on the journey?
- Would you still feel the same level of excitement about the trip?
- Would you consider the flight attendant's behavior professional? Ethical? Why or why not?

Part 2. Now think about the informed consent process for counseling new clients.

Like the flight attendant above, you are:

- new to what you are doing,
- charged with keeping people safe,
- working with all kinds of people: people who are completely new to the experience versus others who have participated many times before,
- establishing the tone/setting the stage for what's to come, and
- required to provide information and education regarding safety.

INDEX

For Product Safety Concerns and Information please contact our EU
representative GPSR@taylorandfrancis.com
Taylor & Francis Verlag GmbH, Kaufingerstraße 24, 80331 München, Germany